JOURNEY TO PROMISE

LaDonna K. Sanders
Kayla Publishing

JOURNEY TO PROMISE

Copyright© 2013 by LaDonna K. Sanders

Published by Kayla Publishing

Guilderland, NY 12084

www.kaylapublishing.com

ISBN# 978-0-615-81860-3

Printed in the USA

Thank you for your assistance in making this Publication possible.

Contributing Writers
Carolyn Cofield
Betty J. Cunningham
Donald Moore, Jr.
Marcia Riley
Mike Servello, Sr.

Publishing Team
Tia Beatty-Transcription
Stella Courtney - Proofreader
Betty J. Cunningham - Biblical Integrity
Jamie Days - Proofreader/Editorial Assistant
Gareth Gilpin – Book Cover Design
Kashawna N. MaCaskill- Proofreader
Reginald P. Sanders, Jr. – Printing Service Consultant

"May the Lord bless you, and keep you: the Lord Make His face to shine upon you and be gracious unto you; The Lord lift up His countenance upon you, and give you peace."
Numbers 6:24-26

Journey to Promise

Preface

Several years ago, I was asked to prepare a short sermon to share in a revival at my local church - Power Realm Church of God In Christ - Kansas City, Kansas. This book is a by-product of that sermon called, *"The Promise Comes through Faith and Patience."* The Bible reference scripture for that message is found in *Hebrews 6:10-12-"For God is not unjust to forget your work and labor of love which you have shown toward His name, in that you have ministered to the saints, and do minister. And we desire that each one of you show the same diligence to the full assurance of hope until the end, that you do not become sluggish, but imitate those who through faith and patience inherit the promises."*

As the author, I invite you to take a short journey with me through scripture and highlighted stages in my life where I have found God to be real and true to His Word. My friend, God is concerned about *every* aspect of your life: the good, the bad and everything in between. You are in His thoughts and on His heart, and you were created to reveal His glory in the earth. The Bible says, in Jeremiah 29:11; that God has an awesome plan for your life. It is my prayer that this discussion will enlighten and encourage you to believe in God, trust His guidance and pursue the Lord and all that He has promised and planned for you!

Yours in Christ,

Minister LaDonna K. Sanders

Chapter 1

Salvation Is Where the Journey Begins

I promise to love you. I promise to take care of you. I promise I will always listen and protect you. I promise to reward your faith, love and trust in me. I promise I'll be with you every day for the rest of your life, and when you make that glorious transition from this earth into heaven, I promise you eternal peace. I promise you paradise, a place free of stress and worry, where fear and pain do not exist, and where turmoil and dysfunction cannot abide. I promise you unending love. This blessing of safety, provision, intimacy, and redemption is available to anyone willing to receive God's gift of love - Jesus Christ. The *Merriam-Webster's Dictionary* defines the term **promise** as **"a legally binding declaration that gives the person to whom it is made a right to expect or to claim the performance or forbearance of a specific action."** In the *Strong's Exhaustive Concordance of the Bible*, the Greek word for a **promise** is *Epaggelia.* One of the suggested meanings is **"a promised good or blessing."** God loves you more than you could ever imagine. You were created to succeed and reign. He wants you to impact this world with good. He wants you to prosper, to be free, and healed. You were put here to demonstrate His love and His glory. God, however, will not force you to believe in Him. He will not impose Himself, or His plans on your life. He will pursue you, and then wait in love, for your response. He will wait for you to make a decision. He will wait for you to seek Him. He will wait for you to choose Him and all that He has promised!

The first man and woman, Adam and Eve, "in one act of disobedience", brought sin into the world and severed man's relationship with God. God out of love for you and I provided a means of reconciliation through the person of His Son, Jesus Christ. Jesus Christ willingly gave His life on a cross, and His shed blood paid the penalty for our sins; erasing our death sentence in Hell (Romans 5:1-13). In John 10:10 – the Bible says that Christ came that we may have life and have it more abundantly; life to the fullest! Promised blessings, strength for the journey, peace, victory and relationship with God awaits any person that would choose Jesus Christ today! Accepting God's gift of love involves confessing with your mouth and believing in your heart that Jesus Christ is the Son of God and that God, in His infinite power, raised Jesus Christ from the dead (Romans 10:9-10). When you believe that whole-heartedly and make that confession, your heart is made righteous; which means **"free from guilt or sin,"** and you are saved. You become born-again; made new on the inside and you are adopted back into the family of God. Your relationship and fellowship with God, your creator, is restored. God places His favor on you, and you have His wonderful promise of eternal life and eternity in Heaven. This promise is outlined in **John 3:16-17 -*"For God so loved the world that He gave His only begotten Son, that whoever believes in Him should not perish but have everlasting life. For God did not send His Son into the world to condemn the world, but that the world through Him might be saved."***

This promise of hope and love is refused by many daily, because we have an enemy, Satan and he is focused and persistent in his opposition against people. His goal is to steal, kill and destroy (John 10:10) what God has created. Satan is after your dreams, your destiny in Christ, your family, your influence and your promise, but Jesus came to give you an abundant life! For the person who has accepted Jesus Christ as Lord and Savior, protection and victory rest in the finished work of the cross. Jesus Christ has done the work. His blood has paid the penalty for our sins. Now, your ability to partake of that victory and everything else promised in God's Word is dependent upon your personal knowledge of what's written in the Scripture and upon your decision to actively believe what has been promised. Faith believes in what God has promised. Faith disregards what it looks like and what it feels like. Faith acts and continues to believe (Hebrews 11:1,6; 2 Corinthians 5:7; James 2:17-20)!

We've all seen those television commercials that guarantee success, wealth, and leaner and more beautiful bodies if we buy the featured CD/DVD series, or the right piece of gym equipment. What some of those commercials fail to mention is that the results, guaranteed by these products, will not happen without choice, commitment, hard work and patience. The Word of God clearly outlines that we will face challenges in this life, but God wants you to be encouraged and trust Him (John 16:33). He is on your side, and He has promised to meet all your needs (Philippians 4:19). God has all power in His hands, and His heart involves bringing you into a place of peace, restoration and rich fulfillment.

Let's talk for a moment about rich fulfillment; purpose, the reason you were created. Have you ever-asked God, why you were put here? Do you sit and say, "There's got to be more to life than this?" Are you trying to figure it all out by yourself? Are you enjoying the gift of life you've been given, or are you just surviving? What about the people in your circle or under your authority, are you helping to make their lives better, or is that even your concern? I've asked myself these questions and more, many times. Am I living the life God intended, and if not, then why not? If Jesus Christ gave His life to rescue me from sin, and give me an abundant life, then there should be a purpose to my living. Along with peace, joy and provision. On my Journey, Jesus found me, and I found purpose. I discovered that I had been given a gift with words; I could take mere words downloaded from Heaven and put them in a play, a poem, a song or a book, and someone somewhere would find hope and inspiration to continue. Someone would recognize that God is real, and His love is true. For me, the ability to share those encouraging words, spoken and written is rich fulfillment, and I am enjoying every minute of my journey with Jesus! My friend, if you're not managing life well, and if you are still searching for purpose, help is available. God's ability to create, manage and sustain is demonstrated in the earth daily. I want you to know that you can trust God! He loves you and is concerned about every aspect of your life. Let's review some of His references: the synchronized solar system in which you live, the sun, moon, stars, and surrounding planets are pretty impressive, I think. What about the beauty and splendor of nature? Have you ever just been speechless, looking at a mountain or the ocean? Take a moment and think about the many different species of animals, plants and insects, and how they coexist. What about the complexity of your internal organs and how those organs work together to keep you alive? Now go, take a fresh look in the mirror, you are an original! Only one you on the whole planet, WOW! Your fingerprints, your eyes, your skin tone, your hair and your physical stature are uniquely yours. Your personality, dreams, aspirations, gifts, and talents were exclusively designed with a specific purpose in mind. Now ask yourself if you seriously think all of this came about by accident or by some big bang theory? Creation itself testifies of God's glory (Genesis 1 and 2; Psalm 19:1-6). God is real. He is the creator of every living thing and His managerial skills have been proven. He loves you and has an incredible plan for your life (Jeremiah 29:11-13)! I believe that there is so much more to be gained from a personal relationship with Jesus Christ than just a "Get Out of Hell" ticket. You can obtain the life you were created to live! You can make the world a better place when you live in constant communion with God, your creator! God wants to bring you into that position of peace, purpose, and rich fulfillment. A life that is filled with sweet communion with Him and Salvation is where that journey begins.

God has given us His Word; the Bible, a book filled with

promises, pledges of goodness, blessings and guidance. Jesus Christ sacrificed His life to restore humanity's relationship with God and made available the promise of eternity in Heaven. The Bible says, "*We have all sinned and fallen short of the glory of God*" (Romans 3:23). Do you believe and understand that? You and I were born sinners (Romans 5:11-15)! Why, not consider freedom, and eternity with Christ? Today, you can be set free from a life of sin and separation from God. Today, you have an opportunity to experience the incredible promise of Heaven and restored fellowship with your Creator. Today, you can begin to embrace purpose, the reason you were created. Sin or freedom, separation or communion, trial and error or rich fulfillment, Heaven or Hell, the decision is all yours! Choose life, choose freedom, choose communion, choose purpose, choose Jesus Christ and consider praying the following prayer: **(Aloud)**

"Dear God, Today, I confess that I am a sinner, and I now realize that my sins have separated me from you. Please forgive me. I believe that your son, Jesus Christ died on the cross, to pay the penalty for my sins, and that same Jesus was resurrected from the dead to restore my relationship with you. Dear God, I make a decision, today,

to turn away from my past life of sin and follow You. I call upon the name of Jesus Christ, and I ask you, Jesus, to come into my heart and life and rule as Lord and Savior from this day forward. Dear God, Help me by your Holy Spirit to follow You, to honor You and to do Your will for the rest of my life. In Jesus' name, I pray, Amen."

During my journey with Christ, I have learned that Life with Jesus works! Jesus Christ filled the void in my soul, healed my heart and gave me purpose! Jesus has been my best friend, my comforter, and my peace. I have learned over the years that if I am going to continue to walk in and maintain the victory and salvation that Christ has afforded me, I must make a daily decision to trust Him, to spend time in God's Word, and time in prayer. God's deserves my gratitude and obedience. He's the reason I'm still alive and sane. I am so thankful to Jesus Christ; He sacrificed His life for my rescue and redemption. He gave me a reason to live! Finding a local church and putting yourself in an environment to hear the preached Word of God is vital. Giving God thanks and putting God's Word before your eyes and in your mouth are most essential to your survival and progress on this "Journey to Promise (2 Corinthians 4:13)." This journey will not be easy, but know that God has promised never leave or forsake you

(Hebrews 13:5-6). God has promised to be with you until the end (Matthew 28:20), and I know from experience that the Word of God has the best advice available on family, marriage, business, health and finance. You will experience days of slow movement, tears and darkness. Honestly, it is just part of the journey. Whatever happens, don't ever stop believing or pursuing Jesus Christ and what God has promised you. Your faith and patience will be rewarded as God's manifested glory unfolds in your life, and salvation is where that journey begins.

Salvation is Where the Journey Begins

Chapter 2

Is Your Vehicle Road Ready?

When preparing for a Road Trip; **a road ready vehicle, fuel and your keys** are a must. In this discussion, the vehicle represents your **faith,** the **fuel** is the Word of God, and your **keys** will serve as the tools or weapons you will need to thrive on this journey with Jesus Christ. God has a tremendous destiny outlined for you. A place of peace and purpose and a road ready vehicle full of Faith is what you will need to bring you into that place of rich fulfillment (Psalm 66:12). In a car or truck, we look for appearance, peak performance and longevity. In life, we look for love, acceptance, significance, stability and longevity. Every vehicle owner knows that regular maintenance, proper fueling and getting needed repairs, will keep your car on the road a lot longer. For humans beings, the love and acceptance we relentlessly look for is found in God and all the information we need to lead successful lives, full of purpose can be found in the Word of God. The Bible is the tool God uses to salvage and repair broken lives. Are you in need of repair? Have you fueled up for the journey? Is your vehicle of Faith Road ready?

The Bible says, *"Now Faith is the substance of things hoped for and the evidence of things not seen"* (Hebrews 11:1). The *Merriam-Webster's Dictionary* defines the term faith as **"an allegiance to duty or a person; complete trust; belief in and loyalty to God."** Faith believes in what it cannot see and makes a heart decision to trust God and His Word and act upon it. This journey with Christ requires faith, and it is absolutely impossible to please God without it (Hebrews 11:6). If we are going to obtain what God has promised in His Word, faith is a must!

In the first book of the Bible; Genesis, God made a promise to a man named Abram. His name was later changed to Abraham. Abraham is considered the "Father of Faith" because he made a personal decision to believe and obey God. In the midst of challenge, trial and crisis, Abraham believed in and waited on the fulfillment of God's promise. Abraham did not waver when faced with difficulty. He continued to believe and obey God. The bible says, "his faith was accounted unto him **(which means credited to his account)** as righteousness **(which means right standing with God)."** We are considered the spiritual seed of Abraham. If we, like Abraham, choose to operate in faith and obedience towards God, then, just like Abraham, God has promised to reward our faithfulness (Romans 4:16-22).

Let's take a closer look at God's initial Promise to Abram:

Genesis 12:1-3-"Now the Lord has said to Abram: "Get out of your country, from your family and from your father's house, To a land that I will show you. I will make you a great nation; I will bless you and make your name great; and you shall be a blessing. I will bless those who bless you, and I will curse him who curses you; and in you all the families of the earth shall be blessed."

The first thing, I noticed in this passage, is that God initiated the conversation. God gave Abram instructions to leave what was familiar to him, his father's home. Abram did not consult with his family or closest confidantes he simply obeyed God. God told Abram that he would show him where to go. During Abram's journey with God, he waited for clarity. He did not take off on his own, but he waited for God to give him the specifics, the next steps. Success, security, and safety can be ours when we too, learn how to wait on God. When God gives you direction and a promise, it often involves a time of waiting. God wants you to be in full agreement with what He has promised. He wants you to be able, to possess and maintain what He has promised. It is important that you learn how to consistently, consult Him and not people for the specifics. Yes, it is easier to seek the advice of a trusted colleague, friend or family member. Yes, we all need expert counsel and prayer support, but when you are waiting on the fulfillment of a promise; seeking direction on whether to marry and who to marry; deciding where to move or work, or engaging in some business or ministry endeavor, God wants you to consult and trust Him! He has the best plan for your life, and He is the only one who truly knows what your future holds (Jeremiah 29:11). God wants you to spend time in His Word, time in prayer and time in His presence so that He can develop your faith. Peace, Purpose, and Heaven are the goal, and God understands that you will need His guidance and strength for the journey ahead. Your faith must be built on the solid foundation of His Word and not on human opinions and rationale. God wants you to have clarity, and He has promised to give you guidance when you ask for it (Proverbs 3:5-7, Matthew 7:23-25). God wants you to learn, *"**Man does not live by bread alone; but man lives by every word that proceeds from the mouth of the Lord**"* (Deuteronomy 8:3). On occasion, your time of waiting will involve fasting **(to abstain from food for a specific period of time)** and prayer (see Chapter 3). In fasting and prayer, hindrances are removed, clarity is given, and courage to obey is obtained (Isaiah 58: 6).

Early in his pilgrimage, Abram meets challenge, but God reaffirms His promise. God tells Abram, "*Do not be afraid, I am your shield, your protection, I am your exceeding great reward*" (Genesis 15:1b). Abram voices his concerns, his heart's desire to God. He states that he is still childless. God responds like any loving parent would respond. God encourages Abram. God instructs Abram to go and look at the vast number of stars in the sky and then says, "so shall your descendants be" (Genesis 15:1-6). God kept His promise to Abraham. The seed of Isaac; the children of Israel; the Jewish Nation are the promised descendants of Abraham (Romans 9:4-9). We are the spiritual descendants of Abraham because we have made a decision to follow Jesus Christ, and we have publicly confessed our belief in Him as the Son of God, and Savior of the world (Romans 4:9-25).

For a more in depth look into Abraham's journey with God; please read **Genesis 12-22** and **Hebrews 11:8-19.**

My friend, the Bible is the fuel you will need to get your vehicle of **Faith** moving, and keep it moving until your assignment in the earth is completed, and you have made that glorious transition into heaven to be with Jesus. The Word of God carries power. When a person hears the Word of

God and receives and believes that word whole heartedly, God releases His power and that person can then receive peace, direction, change and deliverance. This power is mentioned in **Romans 1:15-17-"So, as much as in me is, I am ready to preach the gospel to you that are at Rome also. For I am not ashamed of the gospel of Christ: for it is the power of God unto salvation to everyone that believeth; to the Jew first, and also to the Greek. For therein is the righteousness of God revealed from faith to faith: as it is written, the just shall live by faith."** *(Author Paraphrase)* - Paul, the Apostle is saying, with everything that is within me, I am ready to preach the Gospel of Jesus Christ because I am not ashamed. I am not confused about it in any way. I am thoroughly convinced and fully persuaded that the gospel of Christ is the power, the active force and the tool God uses to produce freedom, deliverance and salvation in the lives of those who choose to believe it.

So you wonder if you have what it takes to obtain the promise. You do, because God has placed within each person the capacity to believe (Romans 12:3). God is the creator of faith. The Bible says, He is the author and finisher of our faith, (Hebrews 12:2) and He has provided the fuel and the means to obtain the fuel that we need to complete our journey with

Him. The Bible says, *"Faith comes by (as a consequence) hearing, and hearing by the Word of God"* (Romans 10:14-17). Getting connected to a local church where the whole Bible is preached and taught will strengthen your faith in God. In a healthy environment, your church family will provide the support, accountability, and encouragement you need to remain faithful to Jesus Christ on your journey.

The Word of God could be considered a multipurpose agent. It is the much-needed fuel for your vehicle of Faith, but it can also serve as a **Cleansing Agent or GPS – Navigation System;** Let's say that you have a personal struggle, you've set aside some time to search the scripture regarding your issues, and you have released those concerns in earnest prayer to God. As you begin, to fill your heart and mind **(reading it, memorizing it and quoting it aloud)** with God's Word on the issue. A cleansing will then begin to take place in your heart because you are allowing the Word of God to wash and renew you inside. The Bible says, *"that Christ also loved the church, and gave himself for it; that he might sanctify and cleanse it with the washing of water by the word"* (Ephesians 5:25b-26). This strategy can be applied to anything; low self-esteem, un-forgiveness, hurt, your health, finances, and concerns over family or business. First acknowledge that there is a problem, and then take those issues to God in prayer. After you have prayed, begin to fill your heart with what God's Word has to say about your problem. God's Word will cleanse your heart and mind, and God will give you the grace, guidance and strengthen you need to walk in freedom (Psalm 46:1).

The Word of God is also conveyed as a **Road Map or Instruction Manual** in righteousness that leads to a complete and profitable life (Joshua 1:8; 2 Timothy 2:16). I have relied on this truth, many times during my "Journey to Promise." God has always been true and faithful to His Word. He will give you the guidance and direction you need. His Word offers wisdom for a better life. Don't forget we are in a spiritual war over souls. Satan is the enemy, and he is focused, and persistent in his endeavor to destroy God's children. Obtaining personal victory on this journey requires that you to have faith in God. Your faith represents your battle shield. The scripture says, *"Above all taking the shield of faith (your trust and confidence in God and His Word), where with you will be able to quench (put out; like water does fire) all the fiery darts (like doubt, deceit and fear) of the wicked"* (Ephesians 6:16).

My friend, God extends His love in the promise of salvation and redemption through His son, Jesus Christ. Faith can be planted and nourished in your heart when you hear, receive and believe the preached Word of God. The Word of God is the multipurpose fuel you will need to reach your full potential in Jesus Christ; that place of peace and purpose. Your vehicle of **Faith** will serve as the transportation, protection and the covering you will need to weather the storms of life. I encourage you to make sure your vehicle is road ready. If you notice during your journey that your vehicle of **Faith** is not running properly, don't keep going, stop and check the road map. Find out what God's Word has to say about your situation. Spend some time searching the scripture and then allow Jesus, the expert repairman, to make the necessary changes and adjustments in your heart, so that you can get back on the road to Promise!

Are you in need of Repair?

Have you fueled up for the Journey, ahead?

Is your Vehicle Road Ready?

Chapter 3

Where Are My Keys?

"Where are my keys, I'm going to be late?" When you're in a hurry, and you've lost your keys, distress and frustration can run high. The schedule of the day can be drastically altered if those keys are not found, and sometimes that delay can result in missed appointments, and missed opportunities. A fruitful life involves staying mobile, and being in a position to embrace God-given opportunities. God has given us keys to access His supernatural assistance and overcome every temptation, trial, or challenge we encounter. He has given us **keys** to keep us mobile. **These Keys; the Blood of Jesus, the Name of Jesus, Obedience, the Word of God, Praise, Fasting, and Prayer** are the tools you will need to keep the enemy (Satan) in check and under your feet (1 Peter 5:8). These keys will help you to reach your promised destiny in Jesus Christ. In this chapter, I will briefly review each key, but our discussion will concentrate primarily on the **Key** called **Prayer**, *my lifeline!*

The Blood of Jesus is a Key

The Bible says, in Ephesians 2:11-13 that we are brought near to God by the blood of Jesus, intimacy between God and man can now take place. The relationship that was broken because of sin can now be restored. Jesus Christ suffered a grueling death by crucifixion on the cross, and the blood that ran from His body bought our redemption from sin, secured our healing, our peace, and our protection from the enemy, Satan. When you believe on the Son of God, Jesus, and confess Him as Lord and Savior, you are then able to benefit from the cleansing and the protection that His Blood sacrifice brings. His blood served as payment for your sin debt. The blood of Jesus gives you a fresh start. His blood washes you thoroughly and makes you new inside. You are made into a new creature full of Hope. The Blood of Jesus covers and cleanses your heart, mind, body, past, present, and future. The Blood of Jesus redeems and restores fully.

As a teen growing up in a Pentecostal church I became particularly familiar with the phase, **"I plead the Blood of Jesus."** It was, and still is a petition for God's protection and intervention. The use of this phrase was adopted and derived from a historical event that took place around 1400 B.C. In the Old Testament book of Exodus 12, the judgment of God was going to be released over the land of Egypt. God advised Moses (His chosen leader for the children of Israel) to take the blood of an unblemished lamb and spread it over the doorpost and lintels of their homes. God explained to Moses that when He passed through the land of Egypt by plague, to strike all the firstborn, both man and beast; and to execute judgment against all the gods of Egypt that the blood of the lamb, spread across the doorpost of their homes would identify the dwelling places of His chosen people. God kept His promise. Protection was granted to the people of God and the destroying plague passed over their homes.

Exodus 12:13-"Now the blood shall be a sign for you on the house where you are. And when I see the blood, I will pass over you; and the plague shall not be on you to destroy you when I strike the land of Egypt."

Today, God has extended a similar request. Jesus Christ is the unblemished Lamb of God (John 1:29). The earth and all it inhabits will be judged one day (Revelations 20-22) and only those whose lives are covered with the precious Blood of Jesus will be protected from the wrath of God. If I were you, I would take full advantage of this opportunity now. I would embrace the Blood sacrifice Jesus Christ has made for you and surrender your life totally to Him. Position yourself for His awesome purpose, and plead for His protection and intervention. Learn how to **"plead the Blood of Jesus."** The Blood of Jesus is a powerful key and the best protection insurance available. It will save your life! Supporting scriptures regarding the power that rest in the Blood of Jesus can be found at the end of this chapter in the section called, *"Hidden Treasures."*

The Name of Jesus is a Key

The name of Jesus could be considered the great divide because most people have absolutely no problem when you mention the name of God. However, when you begin to acknowledge and speak on the name of Jesus Christ, all hell literally breaks out! The dispute arises because some people have bought into the lie that God does not exist, and consequently no need to be concerned with Heaven or Hell. Many others have adopted a belief that their good deeds will earn them entrance into Heaven. My friend, creation testifies of God existents and His Glory, and the only way to enter into a restored relationship with your creator, and obtained the reward of eternity in Heaven is through Jesus Christ (John 14:6). Christians, today and in Biblical times give witness to

Jesus Christ. Many have suffered severe persecution and even martyrdom because their belief in Jesus Christ and their refusal to deny Him. In the Bible, Hebrews 11:32-35 gives an example of how many Christians maintained their faith in God and refused temporary relief, opting for a better resurrection at Christ's return. These people understood that Jesus was the Messiah, the Savior of the world, and they embraced the sacrifice He made for them. Jesus Christ, the Son of God erased our death sentence in hell and secured our everlasting redemption and our escape from eternal damnation, in his suffering, crucifixion and resurrection.

John 14:1-6-"Let not your heart be troubled; you believe in God, believe also in Me. In My Father's house are many mansions; if it were not so, I would have told you. I go to prepare a place for you. And if I go and prepare a place for you, I will come again and receive you to Myself; that where I am, there you may be also. And where I go you know, and the way you know." Thomas said to Him, "Lord, we do not know where You are going, and how can we know the way?" Jesus said to him, "I am the way, the truth, and the life. No one comes to the Father except through Me."

Hebrews 11:32-35- "And what more shall I say? For the time would fail me to tell of Gideon and Barak and Samson and Jephthah, also of David and Samuel and the prophets: who through faith subdued kingdoms, worked righteousness, obtained promises, stopped the mouths of lions, quenched the violence of fire, escaped the edge of the sword, out of weakness were made strong, became valiant in battle, turned to flight the armies of the aliens. Women received their dead raised to life again. Others were tortured, not accepting deliverance, that they might obtain a better resurrection."

When we say, **"In Jesus' name,"** It is a simple act of reverence, an acknowledgment of the authority that Jesus Christ has been given in heaven, earth and in our lives as believers. It's about honor, obedience and understanding the authority in His name (John 14:13-14). When our prayer petitions are in line with God's written word, and we make a decision to believe God's Word, obey His request and trust in the authority found **"In Jesus' name,"** we can be confident that our prayers will be answered. The **name of Jesus** is like a King's signet on a document or like the President's signature on a law. It is irrefutable and unchangeable! Use the **"name of Jesus,"** it's one of your keys. Reverence the authority in His name, obey God and watch the Lord, God, Almighty intervene on your behalf, **"In Jesus' name!"** Additional supporting scriptures regarding the **name of Jesus** can be found in the section called *"Hidden Treasures"* at the end of this chapter.

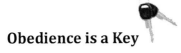

Obedience is a Key

The *Merriam-Webster's Dictionary* defines the term **temptation** as *"a cause or occasion of enticement especially to evil."* Temptation is anything and anybody that would draw you away from God's present will and plan for your life. Many times your desires are genuine, but the timing in which God wants to bring those things into your life is the conflict. Praying for daily guidance, seeking God for the specifics, and then obeying His directives will help you stay on the right path (Proverbs 3:5-7; Jeremiah 29:11-14). If you are going to overcome temptation you must remember three things:

1. *Temptation does not come from God.*

> *James 1:13-15-"Let no one say when he is tempted, "I am tempted by God"; for God cannot be tempted by evil, nor does He Himself tempt*

27

anyone. But each one is tempted when he is drawn away by his own desires and enticed. Then, when desire has conceived, it gives birth to sin; and sin, when it is full-grown, brings forth death."

2. *The Lord is willing and able to help you, when you ask for it.*

> **I Corinthians 10:13-"No temptation has overtaken you except such as is common to man; but God is faithful, who will not allow you to be tempted beyond what you are able, but with the temptation will also make the way of escape, that you may be able to bear it."**

3. *What should, I as a Christian do in the midst of trial and temptation?*

> Show God how much you love him by your actions and your attitude, yield to Him and obey His request on your life. Your actions, attitude and obedience all service as resistance against your enemy (Satan). Imitate Jesus! Learn how to check the devil with the Word of God (Matthew 4:1-11).

John 14:15-18-"If you love Me, keep My commandments. And I will pray the Father, and He will give you another Helper, that He may abide with you forever—the Spirit of truth, whom the world cannot receive, because it neither sees Him nor knows Him; but you know Him, for He dwells with you and will be in you. I will not leave you orphans; I will come to you."

James 4:7-8-"Therefore submit to God. Resist the devil and he will flee from you. Draw near to God and He will draw near to you. Cleanse your hands, you sinners; and purify your hearts, you double-minded."

I Peter 5:9-10-"Resist him, steadfast in the faith, knowing that the same sufferings are experienced by your brotherhood in the world. But may the God of all grace (undeserved favor), who called us to His eternal glory by Christ Jesus, after you have suffered a while, perfect (make whole and complete), establish, strengthen, and settle you."

The Word of God is a Key

The **Word of God** is a key that carries creative power. It will turn your mourning into praise, and your broken dreams, into new beginnings. The Word of God will bring peace, wisdom, sound reasoning and right decisions to a lost and troubled mind. The Word of God will usher tangible healing into your heart and body. When you learn how to use this key correctly it will put Satan on the run and reminding him that God has the control dial in your life. Whatever God says shall come to pass. The Word of God will save, heal, guide and bring about the necessary changes you need to live a prosperous and purpose filled life on earth. Let's take a look at what God has to say about His Word!

Isaiah 55:10-11-"For as the rain comes down, and the snow from heaven, And do not return there, But water the earth, And make it bring forth and bud, That it may give seed to the sower and bread to the eater, so shall My word be that goes forth from My mouth; It shall not return to Me void, but it shall accomplish what I please, And it shall prosper in the thing for which I sent it."

John 6:63-"It is the Spirit who gives life; the flesh profits nothing. The words that I speak to you are spirit, and they are life."

2 Timothy 3:15-17-"And that from childhood you have known the Holy Scriptures, which are able to make you wise for salvation through faith which is in Christ Jesus. All scripture is given by inspiration of God, and is profitable for doctrine, for reproof, for correction, for instruction in righteousness, that the man of God may be complete, thoroughly equipped for every good work."

The importance of the Word of God in the life of a believer is referenced in Chapter 2.

Praise is a Key

Praise is defined in *Merriam-Webster's Dictionary* as, **"the act of expressing approval or admiration; the offering of grateful homage in words or song, publicly and enthusiastically."** God is exalted, lifted up, magnified, made big and enthroned in our praise. Our praise welcomes God's presence into our world, and invites Him to rule and reign over our natural affairs. We do not praise to manipulate God.

We praise God because He is worthy of our adoration. We praise God because He is merciful and forgiving. We praise Him because He is the Creator, and His gracious intervention in our lives rescued us from doom! Pastor Elvin Rhone Jr., says, "Our praise dismantles and shakes up everything the enemy is trying to set up in your life. Our praise is like an earthquake to Satan's plots and schemes against us. Our praise shuts him down (Psalm 8:2)!" **Praise** is a tool, a weapon and a **Key** that you can use to invite God's reign in your present situation. **Praise** brings strengthen, secures our freedom, and victory when under attack from the enemy. **Praise** is a **key** that can be used to lift heavy hearts. Let's take a look at what God's word has to say about **Praise**:

Psalm 8:2–"Out of the mouth of babes and nursing infants You have ordained strength, Because of your enemies, that you may silence the enemy and the avenger."

Psalm 22:3-4-"But You are Holy, Enthroned in the praises of Israel. Our fathers trusted in You; They trusted and You delivered them."

Isaiah 61:3–"To appoint unto them that mourn in Zion, to

give unto them beauty for ashes, the oil of joy for mourning, the garment of praise for the spirit of heaviness; that they might be called trees of righteousness, the planting of the Lord that he might be glorified."

Additional supporting scriptures regarding **Praise** can be found in the section called *"Hidden Treasures"* at the end of this chapter.

Fasting is a Key

Fasting means to abstain from food for a specific period of time; **fasting,** coupled with prayer helps facilitate Godly change, from our old nature to God's way of living. In the Old Testament Scripture, Isaiah 58:5, we are taught that **fasting** is a tool or key used by God, to break bands of wickedness, and negative, death producing patterns in our lives and the lives of others. Fasting is the key used to set us free from heavy burdens brought on by the cares of this life and circumstances that are sometimes a result of our own decisions. Fasting frees us from oppression, yokes and ties that bind us to our old master, Satan, and our old sinful nature.

Isaiah 58:5-6- "Is it such a fast that I have chosen? A day for a man to afflict his soul? Is it to bow down his head as a bulrush, and to spread sackcloth and ashes under him? Wilt thou call this a fast, and an acceptable day to the LORD? Is not this the fast that I have chosen? To loose the bands of wickedness, to undo the heavy burdens, and to let the oppressed go free, and that ye break every yoke?"

In the *Strong's Exhaustive Concordance of the Bible,* the Greek word for **FAST** is *Twot.* It means **to abstain from food.**

We were all born sinners, and we live in a world that offers many daily enticements to sin. Prior to receiving Jesus, as Lord and Savior, most of us willingly participated in sins that produced negative patterns in our lives. In accepting Jesus Christ as Lord and Savior, our hearts are made clean and new. However, abandoning our old way of thinking, handling money, people, situations, relationships and learning how to do things God's way is a process. That process is walked out on this "Journey to Promise."

Mature Christians have learned how to say "no" to self. The bible calls this: "dying to self or crucifying your flesh." *Romans 8:13-"For if you live according to the flesh you will die; but if by the spirit you put to death the deeds of the body, you will live."* Christian maturity also involves understanding that how you previously appeased your fleshly desires and pursued getting your needs met, has to be completely abandoned, and God's way embraced. My friend, this "Journey to Promise" requires change; and some of that change begins with learning how to say "no" to self and "yes" to God's best. **Fasting** facilitates the changes, and adjustments needed in our lives, to make us more like Christ.

In the following Old Testament Scripture, we see an example of how fasting produced courage, protection, clarity and direction.

> *Ezra 8:21-23-"Then I proclaimed a fast there at the river of Ahava, that we might humble ourselves before our God, to seek from Him the right way for us and our little ones and all our possessions. For I was ashamed to request of the king an escort of soldiers and horsemen to help us against the enemy on the road, because we had spoken to the king, saying, "The hand of our God is upon all those for good who*

seek Him, but His power and His wrath are against all those who forsake Him." So we fasted and entreated our God for this, and He answered our prayer."

In the following New Testament Scripture, we are taught that fasting should be private.

> *Matthew 6:16-18-"Moreover, when you fast, do not be like the hypocrites, with a sad countenance. For they disfigure their faces that they may appear to men to fast, anoint your head and wash your face, so that you do not appear to men to be fasting, but to your Father who is in the secret place; and your Father who sees in secret will reward you openly."*

In the following New Testament Scripture, Jesus conveys that some things are only resolved through prayer and fasting. Fasting and prayer can produce resolution and deliverance!

> *Mark 9:23-29-"Jesus said unto him, If thou canst believe, all things are possible to him that believeth. And straightway the father of the child cried out, and said with tears, Lord, I believe; help thou mine unbelief. When Jesus saw that the people came*

running together, he rebuked the foul spirit, saying unto him, Thou dumb and deaf spirit, I charge thee, come out of him, and enter no more into him. And the spirit cried, and rent him sore, and came out of him: and he was as one dead; insomuch that many said, He is dead. But Jesus took him by the hand, and lifted him up; and he arose. And when he was come into the house, his disciples asked him privately, Why could not we cast him out? And he said unto them, This kind can come forth by nothing, but by prayer and fasting."

In the Old Testament chapter, **Isaiah 58,** God clearly states what is and is not an acceptable **Fast.** Apart from denying yourself of food and other things, this chapter goes on to say that praying for personal holiness and deliverance, obeying God, offering God pure and sincere worship, and meeting the needs of the poor, the needy, and the oppressed will make your fasting effective and acceptable to God.

Prayer is a Key

The *Merriam-Webster's Dictionary* defines the term prayer as **"an address, petition or request to God."** Human beings have been given the awesome gift of communicating with God. We have not been left to play trial and error with our lives. We can choose to consult the Lord. We can include Him in our decisions. We can ask for His guidance and then wait to receive instructions from a God who knows, everything about everyone. Or, we can attempt to do it all on our own. Let me share a little something with you, God is waiting to hear from you (Jeremiah 33:3)! He wants to bless your life and **Prayer** is a **Key** that will unlock those blessings.

Find your keys and use the **key** called prayer, regularly. I guarantee it will help you get to your personal place of promise. Jesus taught His disciples to pray. He encouraged them to reverence and worship God, the Father, and to ask God for protection, forgiveness, provision and guidance daily. Jesus taught His disciples to forgive others, to seek God for deliverance from all that is evil, and to ask God to reveal His power and glory in the earth, just as it is displayed in heaven (Matthew 6:9-13). Here are a few Biblical examples of prayer and faith at work in the earth. The Old Testament book of 1 Chronicles 4 outlines a story about a man name Jabez. Jabez was a descendant of the tribe of Judah. He is described in the scripture as a man more honorable than all his brothers. His mother gave him this particular name because she experienced extreme pain during his childbirth. She called him Jabez, which means, *"He will cause Pain."* This was a curse. The people of that day believed that this verbal confession would distill into human reality. One sincere prayer of faith from Jabez changed his life completely. Jabez asked God for unlimited goodness and favor, and for influence in the earth. He asked God to allow His presence and power to flow in his life. Jabez asked God to protect him from any evil that others might attempt to do to him and to keep him from participating in evil. He did not want to cause others pain. The Bible records that God granted his request. This prayer ushered the blessings of God into his life, reversed the curse and restored his dignity.

1 Chronicles 4:9-10–"Now Jabez was more honorable than his brothers, and his mother called his name Jabez saying, "Because I bore him in pain." And Jabez called on the God of Israel saying, "Oh that You would bless me indeed, and enlarge my territory, that Your hand would be with me, and that You would keep me from evil, that I may not cause pain!" So God granted him what he requested."

Our second example of prayer and faith in the earth is about a lady named Hannah. Hannah was the wife of Elkanah. The Bible says in **I Samuel 1** that Elkanah loved Hannah, despite the fact that she was barren. In the Old Testament, people viewed barrenness as a curse from God. Hannah was grieved and taunted by other women because of her inability to have children. Hannah had a desire to give her husband a male child, and she made her request known to God. During one visit to the tabernacle of the Lord with bitterness of soul, Hannah prayed and wept in anguish. She made a vow to God that if He would give her a male child, she would give him back to the Lord all the days of his life, and no razor would touch his head. The scripture records, the next day Elkanah and Hannah rose early to worship before the Lord and then returned to their home in Ramah. Elkanah and Hannah spent some intimate time together, and the Lord remembered her. Hannah conceived, bore a son, and named him Samuel. God gave Hannah the desire of her heart. He answered her prayers and blessed her with son and blessed the nation of Israel with a true Prophet (1 Samuel 1).

I Samuel 3:19-20-"So Samuel grew, and the Lord was with him and let none of his words fall the ground. And all Israel from Dan to Beersheba knew that Samuel had been established as a prophet of the Lord."

The last example of prayer and faithfulness in the earth is about Daniel, one of several young men taken captive by Nebuchadnezzar, King of Babylon when Jerusalem was invaded. The scripture tells us that, as a youth, Daniel had great reverence for God. Daniel, although captive in a strange land, had purposed in his heart not to defile himself. The Bible says that God gave Daniel knowledge, skill in literature, wisdom, and the ability to understand visions and dreams. All of these things caused him to be chosen to serve before the king (Daniel 1). When the Babylon kingdom was taken over in 539 B.C., Darius, the Mede, assigned Daniel to be one of three governors over the whole kingdom. Daniel distinguished himself above the other governmental leaders. He possessed an excellent spirit and was faithful to God and the king. The king had even given thought to set Daniel over the whole kingdom. This caused his peers to be extremely jealous. In their jealousy, they consulted together to establish a statue and a decree stating that anyone found praying to any god or man, except the king, for the next thirty days, would be thrown into the den of lions. Daniel remained faithful to God. He continued to pray and thank God, despite the decree of death. Daniel believed God in the midst of danger and crisis, and God preserved his life. The scripture goes on to tell us that King Darius commanded two things: First, a new decree was to be issued stating that, in every dominion of his kingdom, men must tremble and fear before the God of Daniel. Secondly, that Daniel's enemies, with their wives and children, were to be casted into the den of lions (Daniel 6). I don't think these men thought about the consequences or the trouble that would unfold in their lives when they made a conscious decision to plot against, Daniel, a righteous man of God.

Daniel 6:10- "Now when Daniel knew that the writing was signed, he went home. And in his upper room, with his windows open toward Jerusalem, he knelt down on his knees three times that day, and prayed and gave thanks before his God, as was his custom since early days."

Daniel 6:16- "So the king gave the command, and they brought Daniel and cast him into the den of lions. But the King spoke, saying to Daniel, Your God, whom you serve continually, He will deliver you."

Daniel 6:21-23- "Then Daniel said to the king, "O king live forever! My God sent His angel and shut the lions mouths, so that they have not hurt me, because I was found innocent before Him; and also, O king, I have done no wrong before you." "Now the King was exceedingly glad for him, and commanded that they should take Daniel up out of the den. So Daniel was taken up out of the den and no injury whatever was found on him, because he believed in his God."

Jabez, Hannah and Daniel, all needed something from God. They understood their human limitations and knew that only God could grant their request. Jabez was given dignity, made distinguished and upright far above his brothers because he asked God to reverse the curse. Hannah, in her desperate desire for a child, made a request of the Lord and God blessed her with a son and blessed the whole nation of Israel with a true prophet. Finally, Daniel, the government leader, was kept from destruction and even played an instrumental part in changing government law because he made a decision to stand for righteousness. He continued in his lifestyle of prayer and remained faithful to God, despite the opinions and threats of men.

Prayer is necessary, important and powerful in the life of a believer. ***Prayer*** *is my lifeline!* I know exactly where I'd be without it; dead, in a grave somewhere. The Lord taught me to pray. The Lord made me strong and set me free from a past filled with low self-esteem, fear, failure and domestic violence. Whether the need is forgiveness, healing, provision, guidance or protection, God waits for us to pray. He looks for an invitation to reign on our behalf. He wants to heal our land and Prayer is a powerful the Key. *2 Chronicles 7:14 -"If My people who are called by My name will humble themselves, and pray and seek My face, and turn from their wicked ways, then I will hear from heaven, and will forgive their sin and heal their land."* When things seemed dark and hopeless, when physical sickness came to visit, and the residue of divorce, rejection, violence and depression wanted to linger, I held on to and put into practice a verse of scripture I learned as a child - *Luke 18:1-"and he spake a parable unto them to this end, that men ought always to pray and not faint."*

My spiritual heritage is rooted in prayer. My maternal aunts; Missionary Leola Caldwell-Jones **(a Church Mother),** Missionary Mable Caldwell-Stevenson **(a Pastor's wife),** and Missionary Mandy Caldwell-Thomas **(a Pastor's wife)** seem to be especially graced in this area. I watched these women pray for their parents, family members, church families, and neighbors. Many of my childhood memories revolve around family gatherings and prayer meetings. Several existing churches in Northeastern Louisiana and in other parts of the United States have been birthed because these women unselfishly prayed. Several members of my family are presently serving as Pastors, Elders, Evangelists, Ministers, Engineers, Educators, Musicians, Entrepreneurs, and Caregivers because these women and others in my family took the time to pray. They sought God for the protection and salvation of the Caldwell descendants. Because of prayer, I have family members who have been preserved through war, malicious shootings, tragic vehicle accidents and thoughts of suicide. If you have been praying for a parent, a spouse, a wayward child, a friend or a loved one, don't stop praying! Time and God are on your side, and your miracle is on the way! In my teens, I watched my 70+ year-old maternal grandparents **(Doc and Jellean Caldwell)** make a decision to trust Jesus Christ as Lord and Savior. These two alert, able-bodied, elderly, kind hearted, church going, good-natured people made a decision for Jesus Christ. My friend, God hears and answers prayer! So talk to Him, use your **Keys**, your family's peace, protection, provision and salvation depends on it!

James 5:13-16-"Is anyone among you suffering? Let him

pray. Is anyone cheerful? Let him sing psalms. Is anyone among you sick? Let him call for the elders of the church, and let them pray over him, anointing him with oil in the name of the Lord. And the prayer of faith will save the sick, and the Lord will raise him up. And if he has committed sins, he will be forgiven. Confess your trespasses to one another, and pray for one another, that you may be healed. The effective, fervent prayer of a righteous man avails much."

God Hears and Answers Prayer

In the summer of 2005, I began making several trips to the Emergency Room for chest pains. The diagnosis was always the same. It was extreme anemia and stress. After about the fifth Emergency Room (ER) visit and several trips to three different doctors, who all seem to be playing trial and error with my life, health and money, I realized it was past time to consult the Lord for clarity and direction. Being new in the city, I went straight to my insurance carrier booklet and cut out the names of three female physicians. I stuck the list in my Bible and asked the Lord to help me find the right doctor. After a few weeks of prayer, early one morning, I began hearing the name "Marin." Then I remembered "Marin" was one of the names on the physician's list in my Bible. I called the office, talked briefly with her receptionist who just happened to be a local pastor (Pastor Shirley Daniels) in the city, about my situation and then made an appointment with Dr. Josefina Vega Marin. Upon my first visit, she ordered several tests, most of which had never been done before. The results indicated that I had an extremely large tumor. The issue had been identified, Praise the Lord!

Now what? One evening, shortly after a Magnetic Resonance Imaging (MRI), and during my personal prayer time, I began to understand that I was going to have to walk through something. I was not really sure what, or how extreme it would be, but I knew that this was not going to be one of those situations where God just removed the tumor. I found comfort in two things. First, a personal knowledge, or reference of God's healing power. Secondly, a scriptural promise from the Word of God that I would live and that He would never leave nor forsake me.

Psalm 118:16-18-"I shall not die, but live and declare the works of the Lord."

Hebrews 13:5b-"I will never leave nor forsake you."

During this health crisis, I gained a greater understanding of God's love and sovereignty. This divine connection was a result of God's concern for my life and a part of His plans to restore my health. Dr. Josefina Vega Marin and her receptionist, Pastor Shirley Daniels, met me with hugs, expert medical care, prayer, and words of wisdom. My life has been extended and enriched by having met these two wonderful women. We became friends and sisters in Christ during this crisis. They held my hands and walked with me through the valley of the shadow of death. On July 7, 2006, Surgeon, Dr. Josefina Vega Marin removed a tumor weighing over 18 pounds and approximately 12 inches long. The pathology report revealed no cancer. Hallelujah! Praise God for modern medicine, gifted doctors and women who are not afraid to pray. I am a living witness that God hears and answers prayer!

My friend, this journey will include many changes, challenges, and surprises but have no fear, God has promised to be with you every step of the way. He is a God that hears and answers prayer. So find your **Keys** -**The Blood of Jesus, the Name of Jesus, Obedience, the Word of God, Praise, Fasting and Prayer,** and learn how to use your tools. Your mobility, your success, your family's protection and salvation are at stake and your promised destiny waits!

Hidden Treasures
Additional Supporting Scriptures

The Blood of Jesus

Ephesians 2:11-13   Hebrews 9:13-1

I John 1:6-8   Revelations 12:11

The Name of Jesus

John 14:13-14   Acts 4:9-12

Philippians 2:9-11   Colossians 3:17

Obedience

Deuteronomy 28:1-10   I Samuel 15:22

Psalms 5:4-8   Matthew 4:1-11

Romans 6:14-18   Hebrews 5:7-9

1 Corinthians 15:57-58   2 Corinthians 10:3-6

Praise

Psalm 63:4   Psalm 95:1-6

Psalm 47:1   Psalm 50:23

Psalm 40:3   Psalm 116:17

1 Chronicles 13:8   Psalms 100

Chapter 4

Patience is the Road

"My brethren, count it all joy when you fall into various trials, knowing that the testing of your faith produces patience. But let patience have its perfect work, that you may be perfect and complete, lacking nothing."

James 1:1-5

The *Merriam-Webster's Dictionary* defines the term **patience** as **"the bearing of provocation, annoyance, misfortune, or pain without complaint, loss of temper, irritation, or the like. An ability or willingness to suppress restlessness or annoyance when confronted with delay."** In the *Strong's Exhaustive Concordance of the Bible,* the Greek word for **patience** is *Makroyumia* which means **"enduring with calmness; quiet suffering; with long enduring temper; firmness of mind to encounter danger or to bear pain or adversity; perseverance and steadfastness."** Patience is not an inherited virtue. It is a character trait that is developed when you experience challenge and difficulty, and you refuse to quit or surrender to doubt and complaint. Patience is the fruit of the Holy Spirit working in your life. Loyal ambassadors and mature believers are groomed, molded and shaped on this road called Patience. They emerge as men and women who have learned how to trust and obey God and who are not afraid to tell others about His Love. Personal growth, Christ-likeness, wholeness, intimacy with Jesus Christ and clarity of purpose can be obtained on the road called Patience. Avoid it and you could miss out on a big blessing!

STORMS

Everyone loves to travel when the sky is clear, the sun is out, and the road is dry. Even a long road trip can be fairly enjoyable when the weather is good. In life and especially on this "Journey to Promise" you will experience seasons of change similar to our natural weather. When you encounter personal storms like sickness, wayward children, marital and financial distress, betrayal, and disappointment; staying on the right path and holding on to hope can become very difficult. The severity and length of any storm can leave you feeling vulnerable and interfere with your vision, making it hard to see the road ahead, or follow previously given directions. Experienced vehicle drivers and mature Christians have learned to take extra precautions when traveling through a storm. Vehicle drivers turn on their high beam lights, and drive slower so that they can pay closer attention to the road. Sometimes, they'll ask passengers to be quiet and even silence the radio, all to eliminate distractions because they understand staying focused and alert can be a matter of life and death. I have learned how to take extra precautions during my personal storms. Identifying distractions and being on guard against time robbers can help you stay the course. Searching for and mediating on scriptures that pertain to my problems and spending time in God's presence; in prayer and worship, has kept from being pulled into activities that have nothing to do with God's purpose and direction for my life. When I began this journey with Jesus Christ, I got sidetracked a lot and I did a lot of crying. I found that storms, often uncovered my impurities, surfacing hidden attitudes and behaviors that needed to be uprooted out of my life. It took awhile, but I have learned how to be honest with God about my struggles, fears, mistakes and sin. Acknowledging my issues, asking for God's help, and repenting of my sins opened the door for healing, wholeness and restoration in my life. Today, I cry a little less, and when the road seems dark, and the winds are heavy, now I sing and pray in the eye of the storm. Deliberately and consistently applying God's word to my life situations, and patiently waiting in faith for His guidance and intervention has become a daily practice. On this road called Patience, the Lord taught me to pray, caused me to live, and made me stronger. During my storms of abuse, rejection, injury, poverty, loneliness, and sickness, I held dear two scriptures I learned as a child:

Isaiah 41:10 – "Fear thou not; for I am with thee: be not dismayed; for I am thy God: I will strengthen thee; yea, I will help thee; yea, I will uphold thee with the right hand of my righteousness."

Luke 18:1 – "And he spake a parable unto them to this end, that men ought to always pray, and not to faint;" (KJV)

My friend, I found that God really is a refuge in the time of trouble, and it is His mercy and His grace that will carry you to a place of peace and safety, far beyond the storms of life. Hallelujah!

Today, I will be your Travel Guide on the Road called Patience:

TRAVEL ALERT

Slippery and Dangerous Roads Ahead - Be prepared for

Alternate Routes, Detours, Delays, Road Blocks, and Accidents!

Please Follow Safety and Traffic Signs Ahead

And Don't Forget to Watch and Pray!

TRAFFIC SIGNS

Relinquishing my will and submitting to this part of the maturing and refining process has been the most difficult. Like a strong-willed preschooler, bent and determined to have it her way, it took a few spiritual spankings and several sessions in time out, for me to get an understanding that God is the Boss. It's called making Him Lord of your life. Submission to His Lordship involves doing what you have been asked, not necessarily what you would prefer to do. It's learning how to follow God's instructions; trusting that the Lord knows what's best. Active faith involves following the traffic signs found in God's Word, trusting that your obedience and submission will bring you into all that He has promised. The Bible says that our obedience to God's Word proves our love to Him and that He is Lord in our lives. *John 14:20-21- "At that day ye shall know that I am in my Father, and ye in me, and I in you He that hath my commandments, and keepeth them, he it is that loveth me: and he that loveth me shall be loved of my Father, and I will love him, and will manifest myself to him."*

Let's take a look at a few Traffic Signs I have seen along the road called Patience:

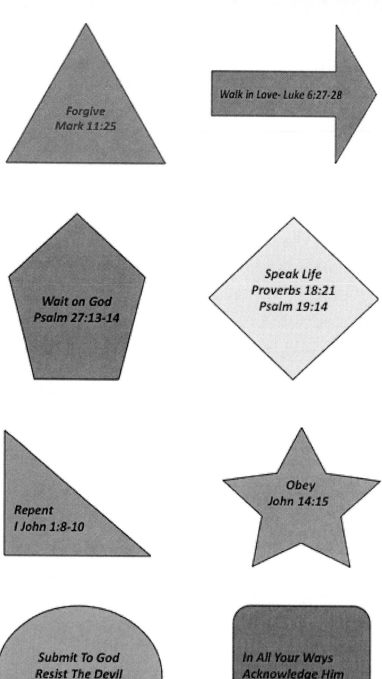

ALTERNATE ROUTES

Humans have been the wonderful gift of choice. It's what makes us different from every other living creature on earth. We can choose to believe or not believe God's Word. We can choose to follow the Lord's lead, and obey, or take our own path into disobedience. The choice is yours, and the consequences or rewards that follow are, too! As a fellow traveler on this road called Patience, I'll confess that I have spent far too many days, tears, and years on alternate routes. Each route ended in some type of loss; a loss of money, vision, energy, time, placement, and respect. I have learned the hard way that it's best to obey God, wait on Him, and follow His path and direction. Obeying the Lord can preserve your life, soul and sanity. Dear Friend, playing trial and error with your life, will never lead you to what you actually need and desire. As your Travel Guide, I would like you to consider the following:

1. God has the best plan. He has designed a path to bring you into your land of Promise. He has everything you need, and His heart's desire is to bless you. He will protect you from your enemies, and His mercies are new every morning.

    Psalm 84:11-12   **Proverbs 3:5-10**

Jeremiah 29:11-14   Lamentations 3:12-25

2. Be conscious of your susceptibility to temptation; understand that you can be easily lured away from God's best when we are offended, weary in waiting or bored. Satan is your enemy, and he will always offer you something he knows you already want.

James 1:13-15   I John 2:15-17

DETOURS

Detours and delays are those unexpected and abrupt surprises that we call tests and trials. It's where the dross **(impurities)** of my life surfaced, not because God wanted to humiliate or embarrass me, but because I needed to see and learn some things about myself. There were places in my heart, and areas in my life that needed cleansing, and healing. When you approach a detour, your options are usually very limited. You can look for an alternate route that may appear to be easier or quicker, or you can follow the detour **(the indirect or roundabout path);** the long way around, accept the delay or quit. Quitting means you have decided to accept defeat, and settle for what you currently have. When you are faced with a test or trial, it is an opportunity to grow. It is where your faith can be strengthened and your patience developed. Ambassadors for Jesus are proven and approved in the segment of the road. During detours; tests and trials, your commitment and loyalty to Christ will be challenged, and your heart motives will be revealed. What you really believe about God and His word will be put to the test. You will find out if you are really trusting God because during a detour or a storm your present circumstances usually contradict what you anticipated. Many times I've asked God questions like:

Lord, why?

What did I do to deserve this?

Are you angry with me?

How is this working for my good?

Is there something wrong with me?

God did I miss you?

How is this fair?

My friend, detours, tests, and trials can position you to receive wholeness, clear direction, and character development. It's where your faith can be strengthened and your patience developed. When you run into a detour on your journey with Christ, don't stress! God is the Master Teacher. He wants you to pass every test. He's already voted for your success and yet He has no problem giving you a re-test. The Lord wants you to grasp the Biblical principles He's laid out for your victory on this journey we call life. He will re-test you until you get it because He wants you to master the material. He is looking for willing souls, people who will commit their time and lives into becoming master craftsmen of His Holy Word and usable vessels of honor for His Kingdom. If you find that, somehow, you have chosen the wrong route or you've gotten frustrated by the delay of your promise, please don't quit. Lean on God, call on Him, and then let Him help you. God's grace and sovereignty will keep you moving on this "Journey to Promise." God wants you to finish strong! Remember, detours and delays cannot be avoided on this road called Patience. Here are a few promises from the Word of God to help you when you are faced with detours, delays, test and trials.

Romans 8:28–"And we know that all things work together for good to those who love God, to those who are the called according to His purpose."

Romans 5:1-5-"Therefore being justified by faith we have peace with God through our Lord Jesus Christ by whom we have access by faith into this grace wherein we stand, and rejoice in hope of the glory of God. And not only so, but we glory in tribulations (testing's), knowing that tribulation produces perseverance; and perseverance, character; and character, hope. Now hope does not disappoint, because the love of God has been poured out in our hearts by the Holy Spirit who was given to us."

James 1:2-4-"My brethren, count it all joy when you fall into various trials, knowing that the testing of your faith produces patience. But let patience have its perfect work, that you may be complete, lacking nothing."

ROADBLOCKS

I, initially, thought that roadblocks were challenges and circumstances that hindered and blocked my progress. I have a different perspective today; I believe some roadblocks were put in place and were permitted to keep me safe. In your daily travels when approach a "road closed" sign, it's understood that the sign is there to protect you from adverse road conditions; such as floods, downed trees and power lines, or damaged roads or bridges. Despite the tears, pain

61

and disappointment I've experienced because of personal roadblocks, I now recognize that some of those closed doors, dissolved business and personal relationships. Even some church rejections were permitted because God was protecting me. God was limiting my choices. The Lord was making His chosen path clear and safe for travel. God wants salvation, peace and rich fulfillment for all of His children. He sets up roadblocks to keep us from traveling into unsafe territories. It can be viewed as a tool of protection against the leeches of life, unhealthy relationships, and unprofitable endeavors. **Roadblocks** keep us from wasting time, money and energy on things that will prove to be unless. God will allow roadblocks to keep you from being destroyed by the enemy. Over the years, I have learned to thank God for the protection, mercy and grace found in Roadblocks because I fully understand that if Satan, the enemy, could have had his way, I would probably be somewhere in a drunken stupor. Financially and spiritually bankrupt, in prison, or yes, even dead by now. Yes, I have taken the wrong path in life more than once. I found myself going down several dark and scary roads. Many of those paths were taken due to my disobedience and impatience. Today, I praise God for the protection found in roadblocks. The following scriptures have become a regular part of my prayer life and are promises I rely on daily.

Psalm 5:8-"Lead me, O LORD, in thy righteousness because of mine enemies; make thy way straight before my face."

Psalm 17:4-8-"Concerning the works of men, by the word of Your lips I have avoided the ways of the violent (the paths of the destroyer). My steps have held closely to Your paths [to the tracks of the One Who has gone on before]; my feet have not slipped. I have called upon You, O God, for You will hear me; incline Your ear to me and hear my speech. Show Your marvelous loving-kindness, O You Who save by Your right hand those who trust and take refuge in You from those who rise up against them. Keep and guard me as the pupil of Your eye; hide me in the shadow of Your wings." (AMP)

Psalm 124-"If it had not been the LORD who was on our side, now may Israel say; If it had not been the LORD who was on our side, when men rose up against us: Then they had swallowed us up quick, when their wrath was kindled against us: Then the waters had overwhelmed us, the stream had gone over our soul: Then the proud waters had gone over our soul. Blessed be the LORD, who hath not given us as a prey to their teeth. Our soul is escaped as a bird out of the snare of the fowlers: the snare is broken, and we are escaped. Our help is in the name of the LORD, who made heaven and earth."

ACCIDENTS

The *Merriam-Webster's Dictionary* defines the term **accident** as *"any event that happens unexpectedly, without a deliberate plan or cause or an undesirable or unfortunate happening that occurs unintentionally and usually results in harm, injury, damage, or loss; casualty; mishap."* People do not plan accidents, or mistakes, but when you are distracted or negligent on the street or in your spiritual walk with Christ, accidents and injuries can occur. Failing to yield to a pedestrian, not stopping at a red light, talking or texting on the cell phone while driving, speeding in poor weather, or in a school zone, can lead to serious injury accidents. On this journey with Jesus Christ, when you fail to guard your heart, or humble yourself and submit to God, serious injury accidents can occur. When you refuse to acknowledge and repent of your sins, refuse to forgive and walk in love, serious injury accidents can occur. When you refuse God's commands or re-direction, serious injury accidents can occur. Sin and disobedience will cause you to suffer mentally, spiritually, physically, and emotionally. In 2009, according to the United States Census Bureau, there were 10.8 million motor vehicle accidents in the United States. To the same degree, I wonder how many people have suffered divorce, strained family relationships, and diminished influence, aborted vision, delayed purpose, spiritual and financial bankruptcy due to sin, distraction and negligence?

In January 1995, in Kansas City, Kansas, I experienced a major injury accident in my spiritual walk. I was emotionally wounded, leaving an extremely volatile marriage. I was recently divorced **(not an excuse),** and now a single parent with a toddler. I started spending too much time with the church deacon. Too, too, too much time with the deacon! I knew better. I broke my own guard rules (Ephesians 4:27), which should have been the first indicator that this relationship was out of line. I compromised my standards, dishonored the Lord and sinned all to appease my flesh. I knew what the Lord was asking of me. In His grace, He had sent a few people to call me into question about this relationship, but I felt like, "Finally somebody to love me, help me, and give me some attention." Despite all the church services, revivals, conferences, and Bible studies, I was still thirsty, still clueless and still searching for love in all the wrong places. In the name of stupidity, I ignored the warnings, and did what I wanted to do. This is what you call absolute disobedience. Then to add insult to injury, out of deception, guilt and shame because I had sinned, I went ahead and got married again – WRONG, WRONG, and WRONG! I should have learned from Adam and Eve's example in the Garden of Eden; that you cannot cover up sin. You may be able to hide some things from people, temporarily, and if you continue in the lie long enough you might even start believing it yourself, but God knows everything. He knows the truth. If you're wise, eventually you will realize that the only thing you can do with sin is acknowledge it, and repent! Then accept and embrace that Christ shed His blood to cover and cleanse away your sins. **Take Note:** The blood of Jesus is the only thing that can cover and cleanse away sin!

Proverbs 28:13-"He who covers his sin will not prosper; But whoever confesses and forsakes them will have mercy."

I suffered tremendous loss. Every aspect of my life was affected, my music ministry as Praise and Worship Leader, my witness and testimony as an Aspiring Missionary, and my position as the Director of Public Affairs at my church. My family relationships, my friendships and my baby boy were all affected by sin. My son was just a toddler and was physically injured by his new stepfather, just a few months into this new marriage. Then in the midst of trying to get out of this ditch, I found out that I was pregnant; a child I later miscarried at 16½ weeks. The entire situation was mentally and emotionally overwhelming. I had unknowingly put my child in harm's way, in search of love. The hurt, shame and embarrassment I caused to my son, family and the church was heart wrenching at times. Understanding that all of this could have been totally avoided made me feel even worst. I was still going to work every day (on light duty because the pregnancy was high risk). I was functionally depressed and angry with myself. My **SIN**, disobedience, and impatience had ushered me into an emotional and spiritual stupor.

Proverbs 13:14-15-"The law of the wise is a fountain of life; to depart from the snares of death. Good understanding giveth favor: but the way of a transgressor is hard."

One evening, about two days before the miscarriage, I was in prayer asking God for forgiveness. It had begun to sink in, that this mess I was in spiritually and otherwise, was a pit that I had dug with my actions and decisions. It became very clear to me that God in His grace and mercy, and out of pure love, had previously rescued me from a very violent marriage, and because of His unfailing love for me and my son, Satan's plan to destroy my life had been halted again.

Psalm 124:6-8-"Blessed be the LORD, who hath not given us as a prey to their teeth. Our soul is escaped as a bird out of the snare of the fowlers: the snare is broken, and we are escaped. Our help is in the name of the LORD, who made heaven and earth."

I've made some bad decisions in search of love, not fully understanding that God already loved and cared about me more than anyone else ever could. It amazes me, but in the midst of all that truth and pain, I felt prompted in my heart to read-*Jeremiah 29:11-14, Isaiah 49 and Ezekiel 36:16-38.* **Wow,** I found God's love and grace in my lowest state. Severely broken, crippled, wounded and at fault, but yet able to hear the Lord speak, amazing! In those scriptures, I found out that the Lord's plans for my life were for good, and His plans for my life had not changed, despite my stupidity. I found out that His call and assignment on my life to reach and teach people about His love had not been cancelled. He was going to get me through this. Yes, the process out of that hole was long and hard, and I have had to deal with a lot of residual consequences behind my decisions, but on July 5, 1995, early evening, I understood that I was forgiven, undeserving but forgiven, at fault and guilty, but forgiven. God was still showing me love, in the midst of the chastening and correction! God, the creator of heaven and earth could have left me to suffer and die in my mess; He could have ignored my request for help, but He did not (Acts 2:21). He had a right to walk away because I had disgraced His name, mishandled His blessings and betrayed His love for another; instead He came to my rescue and spoke words of comfort, hope, correction and purpose. That's the day I recommitted my life to Jesus Christ.

Take a look a few of the scriptures I learned during that process:

Psalm 99:8–"You answered them, O Lord our God; You were to them God-Who -Forgives, Though You took vengeance on their deeds."

Psalm 118:17-19-"I shall not die, but live, And declare the works of the Lord. The Lord has chastened me severely,

But he hath not given me over unto death. Open to me the gates of righteousness: I will go through them, And I will praise the Lord."

Hebrews 12:5-7-"And you have forgotten the exhortation which speaks to you as to sons: My son, do not despise the chastening of the Lord, Nor be discouraged when you are rebuked by Him; For whom the Lord loves He chastens, And scourges every son whom He receives. If you endure chastening, God deals with you as with sons; for what son is there whom a father does not chasten?"

In October 2000, in Tulsa, Oklahoma on one cool, falls morning after dropping my son off at school, I had a major vehicle accident, and again, it was completely my fault. I was driving distracted and preoccupied with life's stresses. I totaled my vehicle. I had to be cut out of the car and rushed to Emergency Room. I had a busted mouth, a broken hip, and later developed a blood clot in my injured left leg. From the beginning, I watched the Lord rally a group of incredible people together to meet my practical and spiritual needs during that long road to recovery. I saw a student on the phone calling the ambulance and asking me if I was all right, immediately after impact. I heard Mr. Mercia, the Assistant

Dean at Victory Christian School, giving the police and medical personnel instructions at the scene, as to which hospital to take me to, and you and I both know where you go to the hospital can sometimes mean the difference between life and death. My friends, Bishop Calvin & Carla Johnson, just hours after the accident, flew my mother into town to be with me. My father called while I was still in the hospital and said, "Tell her not to worry about her next car I got it covered." My friends from a small group, Pat and Robin Loder, while believing God for their first home, paid my rent the first month preceding the accident. My friends and fellow students at Oral Roberts University took my son to school every day for months, kept my hair done, and took me to several follow-up doctor appointments. The Music Department, co-workers and church family at Victory Christian Center bombarded my house with prayers and kept my refrigerator and cupboard full and overflowing. My family from Kansas sent money for utilities and laundry. I gained a better understanding of what it means to be God's hands and feet. I watched the Lord send people to take care of my six year old, and me. Praise God, I eventually learned how to walk again, returned to work, but not school. Nonetheless, my friend and fellow Oral Robert University classmate, Minister Karen Jennings refused to let me walk in fear, she pushing me to get behind the wheel of a car again. (Thanks

Karen!) Remember, I said in the beginning that this accident was entirely my fault. I was a full-time student and a part-time church employee driving distraught and distracted by my full-time bills and single parent obligations. Wow, God showed up again, took care of me, healed my body and changed my perspective about Him, people and life. I will confess, that knowing that a blood clot was in my body was unnerving. Even in the midst of that health crisis, I was constantly reminded of how much God loved me. I stood on His Word for my healing, and God's grace and strength brought about my complete recovery and restoration.

After my vehicle accident in Tulsa, Oklahoma in 2000 and my spiritual accident in Kansas City in January 1995, I watched the Lord hold His hands out to me, just as a parent would while teaching a toddler how to walk. The Lord caused me to live, taught me to pray, and made me stronger. I learned how to walk again in the natural, and I am learning now, how to walk each day with Jesus, being led by His Spirit. The Lord has become my healer, my restorer, my teacher, my best friend, my provider, my coach, my peacekeeper, and my deliverer. He is the Lord, my Redeemer! Yes, some days have been extremely hard, and many days I cried to the point of numbness, but every time that I've felt like giving up, I would hear; *"You are my servant in whom I will be glorified – Isaiah 49:5."* In His love, the Lord was admonishing me to keep moving, sometimes carrying me and holding my hands. Reminding me that I have an appointment with destiny, reminding me that my wealthy place was waiting for me; that place of rich fulfillment and Kingdom fruitfulness.

My friend, this road called Patience is rough and lonely sometimes. Yes, you will have to learn how to deny yourself and say no to self and yes to GOD. My dear Fellow Traveler, if you give the Lord Jesus Christ the opportunity, He will mold you and make you into a sanctified and qualified Ambassador for Him on this road called Patience. Hallelujah! So when you SIN – REPENT immediately! Be honest with God about your struggles and ask the Lord by His Holy Spirit to help you and deliver you! Then renew your mind with the Word of God. Learn how to read and obey the traffic signs found in God's Word and your journey, on this road called Patience, will be a lot smoother and render great rewards.

My brethren, count it all joy when you fall into various trials, knowing that the testing of your faith produces patience. But let patience have its perfect work, that you may be perfect and complete, lacking nothing."

James 1:1-5

Chapter 5

Monuments of Grace and Faith

And we desire that every one of you do shew the same diligence to the full assurance of hope unto the end: That ye be not slothful, but followers of them who through faith and patience inherit the promises.

Hebrews 6:11-12 (KJV)

Monuments are **markers** in history that represent what is notable and great. They are examples of what we've accomplished, how we've overcome and progressed. I have been privileged to work in mega ministry and for three different Pastors in my adult life. I appreciate the exposure and the lessons of faith, excellence, humility, leadership and integrity that I have received. These men and women of God are **markers** on my "Journey to Promise." They have prayed for me and with me in times of crisis. They have encouraged me to hold on to God's Word when circumstances seemed grim. They have challenged me to obey God and pursue His purpose in my life. They are living examples of God's magnificent grace, mercy and faithfulness in the earth. They are *Monuments of Grace and Faith.* I've asked a few of them to share their stories because I believe their testimonies are encouraging. Enjoy!

75

Evangelist Betty J. (Caldwell) Cunningham
* My Mother and My First Bible Teacher*
Retired - Assistant VP of a Bank
Shawnee, Kansas

VICTORY THROUGH OUR LORD JESUS CHRIST

"But thanks be to God, which gives us the victory
through our Lord Jesus Christ."
I Corinthians 15:57

My continual confession of what I have in Christ has built a fortress around my mind. It gives me a pattern of response to every situation and circumstance in my life. The moment a person receives Jesus as their personal Lord and Savior, they also receive absolute victory. I have **Victory** because I have Jesus Christ living on the inside of me. God's Word is filled with promises guaranteeing God's help and provision for our lives.

I thank God that my victory in life has not been dependent upon my ministerial license or degree, nor on any positions I've held. After 26 years in corporate America, I retired, without a college degree, as an Assistant Vice President of a Bank. My victory has not been contingent upon any Sunday school certificates, or perfect attendance awards at Worship

Service. **Victory** is mine because of what Jesus Christ did, nothing more and nothing less. I have victory because of the work of redemption wrought through Jesus Christ's suffering, His death on the Cross-and His glorious resurrection.

The Lord will Provide

Many years ago, I knew nothing about applying the Word of God and waiting on Him. However, I recognized that something was out of order. I worried a lot and didn't have any peace. There were many other things I didn't have. I did have two beautiful children, full of promise, and I always wanted them to have the best. So I talked to my children about God and I taught them to treat people the way they would like to be treated. I encouraged them to keep a job. While raising my children my income consisted of what I earned working a regular job, a part-time job and $66.90 a month in child support. Despite all my efforts, at that time in my life, I still had little to no money left at the end of the month. We had to learn to be resourceful. I remember on several occasions we always had food but no monies for extra things like going to the beauty shop. Perms, roller sets, Jerri Curls, we taught ourselves! This still works for us today.

In my youth, my parents told me, "If you make one step God

will make two." What they were really saying is found in *Isaiah 50:7-"For the Lord GOD will help Me; Therefore I will not be disgraced; Therefore I have set My face like a flint, And I know that I will not be ashamed."* The Lord will help us. One day God gave me a business idea. So I formed a business with my children. I made some business cards and called it – "THE THREE C'S." This company lasted several years. We worked selling grit newspapers, typing documents for others, selling greeting cards and doing light bookkeeping, which included collecting rent for several property owners. Both of my children to this day still operate in some form of entrepreneurial enterprise. Both are still using the clerical and administrative skills they learned in their youth, in business and ministry today.

My first bank loan was $150.00; it was unsecured of course because I did not have any collateral for anything larger. My salary was only $150.00 a week. I had open accounts at several department stores and loan companies, such as JC Penny's, Alders Department Store, Sears, Shoppers Charge, Jones Store Co., Dillard's, Liberty Loan Co. and Grants Department Store. I borrowed money from my life insurance policies to buy school band equipment, Letter Jackets, Special school trips and sometimes just to make ends meet. It's a miracle we did not end up in a shelter, talking about "Miracle on 13th Street", north 57th Street, and a Miracle on 33rd Terrace all in Kansas City, Kansas. Thank you, Jesus! For **Victory** over poverty! God sustained my children and I in times past. Out of His mercy and abundant grace, He brought us to a place of Promise, a place of security, peace and prosperity, found only in Him, a life much different, than when my children were growing up.

Today, I have one visa card which carries a balance well under $500. I have been blessed to give away three working vehicles in my lifetime. I now manage a Senior Living Community that allows me to live rent free with a salary and full benefits. I have learned to save money. Praise the Lord! God is my Jehovah Jireh, the Lord that sees ahead and makes provision. Today, both of my children and I are licensed in ministry. We've been afforded the privilege of sharing the gospel of Jesus Christ and assigned to tell others just how much God loves them! Praise the Lord; we come a long way from $66.90 a month in child support.

Learning How to Walk with God

My road has not been easy. I've walked many uneven paths

and gone down many dead-end streets. I often chose paths that led to "The Bridge Is Out." I have stumbled off the trail many, many times and metaphorically speaking found myself down several dark alleys and up against many roadblocks. For most of them, I had not a clue on how to get around. Some of my choices could be compared to putting a one year old on a ten-speed bike and saying, "Ride baby, ride, to the baby sitters house," a recipe for disaster. Talk about a life out of order!

Sickness had begun to visit, and there were many times I thought surely, "This is it!" Sin was robbing me of my potential and altering my future. Embarrassment wanted to bring me down, and poverty was having its way with me. Frustration and disappointment were my constant companions. Then I began to get my children up early on Sunday mornings, and we would go to the living room and watch a television program called "**The Believer's Voice of Victory**" **– Kenneth and Gloria Copeland Ministries.** I began to read Oral Robert's' book, "**Something Good is Going to Happen to Me.**" Listening and reading material from **Chuck Swindoll** and "**Focus on the Family**" with **Dr. James Dobson,** began to be a great source of inspiration to my family and I. Reading the bible became a daily habit. One of the first scriptures I claimed personally and taught my children is found in ***Isaiah 41:10 - "Fear not, for I am with thee: be not dismayed, for I am thy God. I will strengthen thee; yea, I will help thee; yea, I will uphold you with the right hand of my righteousness." (KJV)*** I posted it on the medicine cabinet mirror and we all committed it to memory. I can truly say, God has done just what He said he would do. He has been our help. He has replaced the spirit of fear with a spirit of Power, Love, and a Sound Mind (2 Timothy 1:7). He has upheld us with His Righteous right hand and has strengthened my children and I, and I am so grateful to God for taking care of us.

The Word of God - My Lifesaver

While there are many scriptures that stand out in my life, I will like to take a moment to share a few passages from God's Word that are very dear to me. These are scriptures that I have come to know, understand and apply. They still serve as lifesavers today. I will always embrace **The 23 Psalms – "The LORD is my shepherd; I shall not want."** In life, I have learned that the "Lord is not the Lord's gonna" but "He is" – always in the present.

Ephesians 4:31-32-"Let all bitterness, and wrath, and anger, and clamor, and evil speaking, be put away from you, with all malice: And be ye kind one to another, tenderhearted, forgiving one another, even as God for Christ's sake hath forgiven you."

I Corinthians 10:13-"There hath no temptation taken you but such as is common to man: but God is faithful, who will not suffer you to be tempted above that ye are able; but will with the temptation also make a way to escape, that ye may be able to bear it."

I John 1:9-"If we confess our sins, he is faithful and just to forgive us our sins, and to cleanse us from all unrighteousness."

Joshua 1:8-"This book of the law shall not depart out of thy mouth; but thou shalt meditate therein day and night, that thou mayest observe to do according to all that is written therein: for then thou shalt make thy way prosperous, and then thou shalt have good success."

Luke 6:38-"Give, and it shall be given unto you; good

measure, pressed down, and shaken together, and running over, shall men give into your bosom. For with the same measure that ye mete withal it shall be measured to you again."

The journey toward spiritual growth is an ongoing, day-to-day process. It continues throughout every stage of life, whether you are 20, 30 or 70. We all still have a lot to learn and class will not be dismissed until Jesus returns. Life may not be all that I've hoped for, and some promises have yet to be fulfilled, but this one thing I know-**GOD IS FOR ME!** I remember the past, appreciate the present and celebrate the future because I know the Lord, who holds my future.

Pastor Donald R. Moore, Jr.

My Cousin & Childhood Friend

Pentecostal Powerhouse Church of God In Christ

2120 Minnesota Avenue

Kansas City, Kansas 66102

The New Creature Nature

In the summer of 1995, I was not planning to go to anyone's church. I was talking to my Aunt Carol, and she began to tell me that the family was going to hear my cousin, Damian Caldwell, preach his first message that night. It was a Saturday! Saturday night was the night, I'd usually go out to drink, gamble, and chase women.

So, I get there. It's this little storefront church, right next door to the liquor store. I hadn't seen my cousin in years, and I was really glad to see him in the church. The place was jammed packed. People were praising God so loudly and violently that it just consumed me. My mindset was just to go in for a little while, make an appearance, and then slip out, but I was wrong. I had never seen men praising God the way those men at that church were. Men were crying, dancing around, and thanking God. That was just the praise and worship. Then I heard this pastor say, "You haven't been to church until you've heard the Word of God." That caught my attention again. My cousin, Damian got up. I was in the back, close to the door, and I was going to leave after a few minutes. I had to get to the gambling house. My cousin's message was, **"A New Creature Nature"** taken from *2 Corinthians 5:17.* It says, *"Therefore if any man be in Christ he is a new creature. Old things are passed away and behold all things are become new."*

I realized he was talking about change, about trying something new. Lord knows I needed to change. I was destroying my marriage and running around with the wrong people, who meant me no good. I was trying to be somebody I was not. A so-called Hustler!

The very next thing I experienced changed me. They had an altar call. People were coming up for prayer. Not me. I was just about to get out of there. Then, my grandmother went to the altar. People were falling out under the power of God. My Aunt Carol turned to me, and told me to go stand by my grandmother. I looked at her, and I thought, "You must be crazy, you are closer than I am!"

She just kept on looking at me. Finally, I gave in. I went to the altar to stand by my grandmother's side. It was a set up. The Minister began praying and laid hands on my grandmother's head. It started to feel real hot up in there. She started crying and so did I. The next thing, I knew the Preacher laid his hands on me. I went straight down. I touched my toes with my hands. My feet started back pedaling. My flesh was trying to get out of that place. Soon, there was no one else on the altar but me, and those men that were praising God. The preacher started speaking in tongues. I felt the weights falling off of me. I felt a change. I yielded to the spirit of God and said, "Yes Lord, I want to be saved."

Pastor Donald R. Moore Jr. and his wife, Minister Nikita Moore, pastor a thriving and powerful deliverance ministry called Pentecostal Powerhouse Church of God in Christ in Kansas City, Kansas, where locals and neighborhood residents, have wandered into the sanctuary, "Asking what must I do to be saved?"

Mrs. Marcia Riley
My Friend and Sister In Christ
Wife of Pastor Howard Riley
Tulsa, Oklahoma

STRENGTH THROUGH SUBMISSION

Submission-the act of yielding, obeying or surrendering to the govern of another. -Merriam-Webster Dictionary

As a young girl who was raised by strong-willed, independent woman, I was taught to rely on no one, but myself, for anything. My life and the condition of it were determined by my actions and choices. I was conditioned to stand up for what I believed in and fight for what I wanted. I was not to be subject to anybody and what they wanted. I was taught to be independent! Encouraged to have a 'plan B' when it came to relationships because they very seldom turn out the way you thought they would. My motto was, "My way or the highway, I choose when you hit the highway, you choose which one to take!" It worked out pretty good. So I thought.

I was never one to do what I was told to do simply because I was told to do it. I needed to know every detail; who, when, where, how and why. I felt like everybody had a motive, and if you weren't careful, it would cost you more than you were willing to pay. As you can imagine, this is not a good quality to have when you are married. My husband understood where I was coming from, but struggled with why it was so hard for me to depend on him. I was saved, sanctified and filled with the Holy Ghost, yet I refused to allow him to be totally the head of our household. He had never given me a reason not to trust him. Howard had always taken good care of my children and I. After several years of tug of war in our marriage, the Lord spoke to me and challenged me to relinquish every area of my life to Him (something I thought I'd already done). He instructed me to allow myself to become completely dependent on the husband whom He's ordained for me. I reluctantly agreed to allow my husband to take over every aspect of our lives. This was not an easy transition. It was the hardest thing I'd ever done. It was the complete opposite of everything that I worked so long and hard to accomplish. My independence would vanish.

I reluctantly gave the reins of our family, marriage and finances over to my husband. I prayed for the best. It felt like self-betrayal, relinquishing everything that I stood for. I prayed for patience, wisdom and self-control like never before. I was uncertain and uncomfortable. As the days turned into weeks and weeks into months, things in my life began to change. I realized that I was no longer concerned with what day of the month it was because the bills were due. He was taking care of that. I no longer debated with the children about what activities and places they would be participating in or going to because the decision had already been made. I didn't worry about which repairman or mechanic to call. I just told my husband what needed to be serviced or repaired, and it got taken care of. It dawned on me one morning as I lay in bed, mentally going over my to do list that it all pointed back to him, I didn't have much of anything to do besides let him know what needed to be done. Then I began to reflect back over the past few months and realized how much more joy I had in my life, and how much more peaceful our home had become. I realized how rested and refreshed I'd felt, and how much stronger our marriage had become and wondered why it took me so long to give him the reins! It was at that point the Holy Ghost gently whispered "Strength through submission."

Because I obeyed God and yielded to Him, He had opened doors in my life that I hadn't realized were closed. He had opened the door of freedom from worry and stress. Worry had been evicted out of my life. By surrendering to God, He has shown me that because I belong to Him, He always has and always will take care of me. No 'plan b' needed. My eyes have been opened to things in life, and I have a different outlook than most. I don't complain about what I don't have or what I can't change. I've learned to be thankful for what I do have. I rest assure that Jesus holds me safely in His arms, no matter what this life brings. Patience, love, kindness, gentleness, meekness, joy, confidence and peace had enveloped my life, marriage and family, simply by me becoming submitted to God first, and my husband next...Yes, I surrendered all!!!

Ephesians 5:21-33 - "Submitting to one another in the fear of God. Wives, submit to your own husbands, as to the Lord. For the husband is head of the wife, as also Christ is head of the church; and He is the Savior of the body. Therefore, just as the church is subject to Christ, so let the wives be to their own husbands in everything. Husbands, love your wives, just as Christ also loved the church and gave Himself for her, that He might sanctify and cleanse her with the washing of water by the word, that He might present her to Himself a glorious church, not having spot or wrinkle or any such thing, but that she should be holy and without blemish. So husbands ought to love their own wives as their own bodies; he who loves his wife loves himself. For no one ever hated his own flesh, but nourishes and cherishes it, just as the Lord does the church. For we are members of His body, of His flesh and of His bones. "For this reason a man shall leave his father and mother and be joined to his wife, and the two shall become one flesh." This is a great mystery, but I speak concerning Christ and the church. Nevertheless let each one of you in particular so love his own wife as himself, and let the wife see that she respects her husband."

Pastor Carolyn L. Cofield
My Friend and Mentor in Missions
Founder/Director
Rachel's Tea House
P O Box 4121
Kansas City, KS 66104

The Voice of Rachel
(A Mother's Intercession)

After four decades of marriage, seven children and eleven grandchildren, I could write my own version of the sitcom "Married With Children." In addition to parenting, my husband and I have Pastored several church congregations over a period of thirteen years. Through the years, we have experienced good times, not-so-good times, hard times and happy times, but God has always been good and faithful to our family.

Looking towards the year 2000, we thought we were **Y2K** ready, trusting God to supply all our needs as always. But trouble and adversity came unexpectedly, and our family faced the hardest trials of our lives. After a short bout with sickness, our 20 year-old daughter, Carla, died on January 15. She was a single mom, leaving behind two precious little girls. Hours before her death, I lay praying and crying out to

God near her bedside. My heart was so heavy, overwhelmed with grief, much like the labor and painful travail that I experienced as I birthed her into this world. I began to realize that my broken heart, tears, and pain weren't just for my daughter, who was lying in the ICU at the point of death. I literally felt the weight and burden of prayer for hundreds, thousands, millions of prodigal sons and daughters, single mothers, aborted, abused, and abandoned babies and lost children. God comforted, encouraged and strengthened me for the days ahead with this verse of Scripture: *"In Rama was there a voice heard, lamentation, and weeping, and great mourning, Rachel weeping for her children, and would not be comforted, because they are not (Matthew 2:18)."*

"They (our children) are not" what? They are not at home, not safe in the fold, not serving the Lord, not with their families. They are lost, missing, runaways, scared, confused, incarcerated, on drugs, unwed and pregnant and some prematurely in their graves. It was a cry for the girl next door and for the boy down the street. Someone else's house yesterday, my house today, your house tomorrow. It was too close for comfort – too close to be comfortable.

"For death is come up into our windows, and is entered into our palaces (our homes) to cut off the children without, and the young men from the streets (Jeremiah 9:21)." Rachel mourns, she travails, she weeps, she wails, her heart breaks; she will not be silent, content, or comforted because children are still missing, but no longer missed; for children gone, but not forgotten; for all children, yours mine, ours – everyone – everywhere.

Who is Rachel? Her story is told in the Old Testament book of Genesis. She was a woman, the wife of Jacob, and a mother. She understood what it felt like to be barren, to give birth, and then lose a child. She cried to God, *"Give me children or just let me die!"* Perhaps our culture hardens us to the understanding of this cry of desperation because we pass legislation to kill and abort babies and to save endangered animals and sea creatures.

God heard and answered Rachel's cry. He opened her womb and gave her a son. His name, Joseph, means to "increase" or "to add another." Joseph was later sold into slavery by his half brothers. God answered Rachel's request for another son, Benjamin, but she died after an agonizing childbirth never realizing the destiny, purpose and promising future of her two sons.

Rachel was buried just outside Bethlehem, the place where 2,000 years later, a virgin named Mary, brought forth her firstborn son and called His name Jesus. It was because of this story of Rachel that I began to declare, **"I may cry, but I refuse to give up and die!"** I refuse to waste pain and tears. I believe God bottles all our tears, *"List my tears on your scroll – are they not in your record (Psalm 56:8)?"*

Centuries after her death, Rachel's prophetic voice still cries from the grave. She cried for all the babies and children who would later be killed by the murderous Herod in his attempt to kill the Christ child. She still mourns today for the millions of babies that have been aborted, abandoned, and abused. Like Rachel, for the sake of the children, born and unborn, I refuse to be passive, indifferent, callous, complacent, or content.

We are not to be silent, to be a whisper, to be an echo. We are called to be a **"voice"** To speak up will cost us something, but to be silent will cost us more, the very souls and lives of our families, our future, our sons, daughters, and grandchildren. Every child needs a praying mother, praying parents, praying grandparents, and a praying church.

Since the passing of my daughter, my pain has become my passion, my purpose, my praise and my prayer. Pain is real. God is a pain Reliever, pain Killer, and pain Healer. His grace is greater than our grief. **"Those who sow in tears shall reap in joy (Psalm 126:5)."** In memory of a loved one, some people may plant a tree, release balloons, or write a song or a poem. God desires to give us beauty for ashes, oil of joy for mourning, and the garment of praise for the spirit of heaviness (Isaiah 61:3). In memory and honor of our daughter, we opened Rachel's Tea House Maternity Home & More, an outreach ministry to help meet physical, emotional, and spiritual needs of teens and unwed mothers.

Yes, there is hope! As the women followed Jesus on the Road of Suffering, to Calvary's cross, Jesus turned in compassion and said, ***"Do not weep for Me, but weep for yourselves and your children."*** That day has come according to **Matthew 2:18.** God also gave us a word of hope through the prophet, Jeremiah: ***"Thus said the Lord: "Refrain your voice from weeping and your eyes from tears; for your work shall be rewarded, says the Lord, and they shall come back from the land of the enemy. There is hope in your future, says the Lord, that your children shall come back to their own border (Jeremiah 31:16-17)."*** Jesus is hope for the hopeless and help for the helpless. When we sow our tears, trials and pain into the Kingdom for a greater cause, we will reap in joy a harvest of hope, love, and the peace of God.

Rachel's Tea House (RTH) is a non-profit maternity home, and outreach community program designed to help empower, and equip teen and unwed moms to become productive citizens. We understand the unique challenges young moms face and are here to provide support, tangible resources, mommy training, and encouragement during a time when she needs it the most.

Pastor Mike Servello, Sr
An Excellent Example of Christian Leadership
Founder/ Overseeing Pastor - * My Pastor*
Redeemer Church
931 Herkimer Road
Utica, New York 13503

"Freedom's Journey"
(Sermon Excerpt from – 11-7-2010)

Grace is divine favor. It's divine enabling favor. It's not just favor, but there is also a grace that you and I are to tap into, that enables us to, live a righteous life, a Holy life before God. A life of obedience before God! There is grace for you and I, to obey God and walk with God in a way that is pleasing to Him.

When you receive the Gospel, the power of the grace of God comes and touches your life on the inside and God does something for you that you could never do for yourself; you become born again. What really happens is that you get regenerated; you get a new nature. Something happens on the inside, and the effect of grace is that you get a new heart. Just the way sin worked, now, of all of a sudden, the power of God is working on the inside of you. Now, you are by nature a child of God. There's a new gravitational pull towards Jesus. All of a sudden, there is awareness in your heart that God is real, and God loves me, God cares about me and God is close to me. God stands over you, besides you, saying, "I love you, I have a plan for your life, I'll forgive all your sins." When you receive that gift of love in your heart, you become born again. You are justified, just as if you had never sinned.

The power of the gospel doesn't end when you are justified. When God declares a sinner righteous, He immediately begins the process, of making that sinner more like His son, through the work of the spirit, through the power in His word, and through the involvement of a local church. God peels away our desire for sin, renews our mind and changes our life. This ongoing work is called sanctification, or being set apart. Sanctification is about our obedience, and it does require work. God is calling you to address things in your life and be a set apart believer. He is calling you to walk in a balance of Jesus plus nothing. From the heart saying, Lord, you are the center of my life! I will not substitute anything else. Augustine's quote, "Idolatry is worshipping anything that ought to be used, or using anything, that ought to be worshipped." Here are four questions you should ask yourself: *1) What motivates me? 2) What keeps me going? 3) What do I rely on or comfort myself with, when things go wrong, when life gets difficult, where do I turn? 4) What unanswered prayer or circumstance, would make*

me seriously, turn away from Jesus? In our process of sanctification to become more like Jesus, God wants to deal with these things in our life.

I remember when I first got saved, I had a produce business, it was so difficult, and there was a guy in our church that had a farm stand. I thought that for sure since we're brothers, he would buy his produce from me, and it would put us over the top. I was going to give him a good deal. I could sell to him, cheaper than he was buying. I knew for sure that he was going to take me up on the offer. When I approached him, he shut me down. I was ticked off as a young believer. I went to God. I said, "What is this all about, I can't believe how the church, people in the church, treat you," Then God corrected me. He said, "Who is your source?" "Get your attitude right. It doesn't matter, forget about him." "Keep your attitude towards him right, and keep your attitude towards me right. Don't put any idols between you and me, I will take care of your business." We began to prosper, and I never needed his business. I remember when we first took on our business, it was struggling and on the verge of bankruptcy. It started to grow every year for 5 years. After I got saved it doubled. We were making a lot of money. God has no problem with you making money (3 John: 1-2; John 10:10). I remember a leader came to me and said that business is an idol to you, He said, "Lay it down like the rich young ruler and follow Jesus," Give it all up." That bothered me. I was innocent, and we were the biggest giver in the church. We gave over 35% of the annual income. In many other ways, we blessed the church through our business. I went home, and I was heartbroken. I remember getting down on my knees, *(Thank God for a personal relationship with Jesus)* "I asked the Lord is this an idol? Has this business become so important to me, that I have I been captivated by wealth?" I remember the Lord said to me, "Don't listen to that. That is jealousy!" "He does not have a grid for where you are financially. You have marched off the map financially, but the day will come when I will speak to you to release it, and know this I will give you anything that doesn't stick to your hands. Always remember to put me first." That day did come, not because man told me, but God spoke to me. A couple of years later, the Lord spoke to me and said, "I want you to lay all of this down, give it all up and go into the ministry," I did and my wife Barb cried for two weeks. I took this small church, with only 20 people and $50,000 worth of church debt. When I walked away from the business, my father got so upset with me and said that you are not going to take anything away with you from the business. At the time, my share of the business was worth a quarter of a million dollars, and I was 27 years old and left with only $19.81. I said, OK Lord. I heard your call, God said, "Mike, what you are going to see on your life is my grace poured out." Within six months, all the debts in the church were paid. Supernaturally God began to provide. I remember when we built our second church, in Utica, NY. We were just completing the building. I had a bunch of "Doctors of the Ministry," from a local denomination contact me for an appointment, asking to see our building. There were three or four Doctors of Divinity, all with PhD's and I with no degree. I had a Degree in Kneeology. Kneeology is when you get on your knees and ask God to help you! So they walked through the building and said, "What should we call you?" You can call me Mike. Just don't call me anything bad. They asked, "How did you do this?" I said, "Doctors, we challenged our people to give extra money, and we collected about $600,000 and we mortgaged the rest." One of them said, "What you mean is that you had their annual commitment, what you would call tithing?" I replied, "No doctor, that's not what I mean. They gave their tithes, which supports the on-going work of the ministry. They also gave above their tithes, $600,000." The doctor then paraphrased it by saying, "what you are trying to say is that." I responded, "I am not stuttering, I know that you are much smarter than me. Listen to me carefully, these people gave their tithe and above and beyond. It's called sacrificial giving. They gave $600,000 and now we are in this building," He must have asked me six different ways. He could not understand it, and he was not able to grasp the Grace of Giving. The gentleman could not understand the Grace of God. He said, "Why would people, give that much? We can't even get our people to give 10%," It's called grace something that exist in the heart of people, when the idols are taken out, and Jesus is first and foremost, and they make up their minds that they want to make a difference. When you can earnestly say to God, I am committed to your people, and to extending your kingdom, Let your grace flow through me, miracles began to happen, God responds to us individually.

Jesus the Author and Finisher of our Faith

When Barb and I first got saved, we were saved for only a few months, so sincere, so innocent. I remember, Barb found a lump in her breast. We were young, she was probably twenty at the time, and I was twenty-two, I dropped her off at the doctor's office because I was working. She calls me, and I go and pick her up, and she is sobbing, hysterically. During the office appointment, the Doctor palpitated the lump and drew fluid out because he thought that it was cancer. Now, she is in the car, I am shocked. O my God. I remember I heard a voice, in my heart, say, "so now what are you going to do?" Now you are serving God, What if your wife dies? What are you going to do now? You just gave your life to Christ. It's so bad, and this voice says, what are you going to do now? Is this what you get for serving God?" I remember fear, coming over me, fear thinking what am I going to do? I Love my wife, what am I going to do, I am brand new, I don't have any strength, or capacity to face this, but from deep inside my heart, something came out of my soul. Lord, I trust you, Lord; I have received love and grace. No matter what happens, I will never leave you. No matter what happens Lord, I will be faithful. I will trust you to take care me day by day. You know what, God touched her, and it was fine. What I am saying to you is that decisions are often made, deep, deep in our hearts, when nobody else sees, or hears. There is grace for you. Walk your journey in continual freedom. You cannot control what happens to you, but you can control what happens inside of you.

God's Grace - Then and Now

When my son became ill, many people called me and told me to "confess and just have faith." Confess and just have faith! As much as I wanted to "confess my son is not sick." That was not my reality. I had become shattered by what I was experiencing, and it took days and weeks to clear through, all of the feelings. I also needed to hear from God. Sometimes when you are shattered by what you are going through, it takes time to work through the feelings of anger, denial, hurt, pain and the list goes on. Once I cleared through all of my feelings, I experienced real faith. Real faith is when you not only trust God, but you trust what God says about your current situation. Real faith puts you in the posture to totally trust God. God gave me grace to deal with my son's sickness. God is a Healer, and my son's healing has been progressive. We're a long way from the state of paralysis he experienced at the onset of this illness. God will grace you with the strength to bear whatever you are facing. The Apostle Paul pleaded three times with God to take away the thorn in his flesh. God's answer to Paul was **"My Grace is Sufficient for you!" (2 Corinthians 12:8-10)** In life, the final outcome will not always be what you want it to be. You have no control over what happens to you, but you can control what is inside of you. God will always give you the grace and the strength to bear whatever you have to face. I put my faith and trust in Jesus, and in what He has to say. Believe in Jesus! Believe what He has to say and accept and walk in the Grace of God.

2 Corinthians 12:8-10 -"Three times I pleaded with the Lord to take it away from me. But he said to me, "My grace is sufficient for you, for my power is made perfect in weakness." Therefore I will boast all the more gladly about my weaknesses, so that Christ's power may rest on me. That is why, for Christ's sake, I delight in weaknesses, in insults, in hardships, in persecutions, in difficulties. For when I am weak, then I am strong."

"*And we desire that every one of you do shew the same diligence to the full assurance of hope unto the end: That ye be not slothful, but followers of them who through faith and patience inherit the promises.*"

Hebrews 6:11-12 (KJV)

Chapter 6

Travel Secrets

Saving you Time, Money, and Heartache!

TRAVEL SECRET #1 - CHOOSE TO FORGIVE

Luke 17:1-3-"Then He said to the disciples, It is impossible that no offenses should come, but woe to him through whom they do come! It would be better for him if a millstone were hung around his neck, and he were thrown into the sea, than that he should offend one of these little ones. Take heed to yourselves. If your brother sins against you, rebuke him; and if he repents, forgive him." (KJV)

According to the *Merriam-Webster's Dictionary*, **Offense** is **"something that would cause another person to sin; a stumbling block or a snare."** On your "Journey to Promise" you will be presented with several opportunities to be offended, but in the Word of God you are encouraged to **FORGIVE AND RELEASE OFFENSE!** Un-forgiveness and Offense are in my opinion Blessing Blockers; tools initiated by your enemy, Satan, to keep you from your promise and to lock up your blessings. Jesus died, on the cross to cancel and erase our sin debt. His sacrifice put us in *a position* to receive, a pardon **(forgiveness)** for our sins and God's best: **Freedom, Restoration, Salvation, and Blessings.**

Staying in that place or position of blessings and freedom involves our willingness to forgive others who have offended us. *Matthew 6:14-15-"For if you forgive men their trespasses, your heavenly Father will also forgive you. But if you do not forgive men their trespasses, neither will your Father forgive your trespasses."* When we refuse to forgive others and hold on to offense, we become locked up inside and bound by circumstances. We open the door to broken relationships, barrenness, and ongoing trouble. The enemy loves to use these Blessing Blockers - **un-forgiveness and offense** because he knows it interferes with your mobility and your fruitfulness in the Kingdom of God. Unforgiveness and offense can cause you to miss and abort the plan of God in your life (Matthew 13:20-21).

Matthew 13:20-21-"When anyone hears the word of the kingdom, and does not understand it, then the wicked one comes and snatches away what was sown in his heart. This is he who received seed by the wayside. But he who

110

received the seed on stony places, this is he who hears the word and immediately receives it with joy; yet he has no root in himself, but endures only for a while. For when tribulation or persecution arises because of the word, immediately he stumbles."

On this journey, it is important for you to remember that you are a child of the King, and God sees and knows everything. He knows who did what, when, where, and why. I recommend taking the issue, including your hurt immediately to God! Ask Him to heal your heart, and give you the grace to forgive, and MOVE FORWARD. My friend, I know from personal experience, you can choose to forgive and be assured that the issue will be dealt with. Your Heavenly Father is a God of justice (Isaiah 30:17-19; Isaiah 49:25-26).

Isaiah 49:25-26 -"For thus says the Lord: Even the captives of the mighty will be taken away, and the prey of the terrible will be delivered; for I will contend with him who contends with you, and I will give safety to your children and ease them. And I will make those who oppress you consume themselves {in mutually destructive wars}, thus eating their own flesh; and they will be drunk with their

*own blood, as with sweet wine; and all flesh will know
{with a knowledge grounded in personal experience} that
I, the Lord, am your Savior and your Redeemer, the Mighty
One of Jacob."(Amplified Version)*

Here are Three Things You Can Do to Get Rid of Offense and Un-forgiveness:

1. Be honest, if your heart is hurting, stop pretending that it's not! You know deep, down inside that, you are not at peace with certain people, or organizations because of what they have done, or failed to do. I suggest that you talk to the Lord; He can relate to your pain. He was betrayed by one of his very own disciples. He knows all the specifics and He wants to heal your heart. In prayer, ask Him to purge the sin, pain, bitterness, anger, and un-forgiveness. Ask the Lord to remove it from your heart and help you to walk in unconditional love and forgiveness towards the people who have harmed you. God is waiting to hear from you; He is waiting for you to give him all the broken pieces of your heart because He knows that He is the only one that can make you whole again. God can and will cleanse your heart, and restore your joy, when you are ready to release the past and ask for

healing.

Psalm 147:3- He heals the brokenhearted and binds up their wounds.

I John 1:7-10-"But if we walk in the light as He is in the light, we have fellowship with one another, and the blood of Jesus Christ His Son cleanses us from all sin. If we say that we have no sin, we deceive ourselves, and the truth is not in us. If we confess our sins, He is faithful and just to forgive us our sins and to cleanse us from all unrighteousness. If we say that we have not sinned, we make Him a liar, and His word is not in us"

2. Pray for the people and organizations that have hurt or offended you. Your prayers will help uproot, any negative feelings you may have towards the other person. Honestly, it is hard to stay mad at a person and genuinely pray for them at the same time!

Matthew 5:43-45-"Ye have heard that it was said, 'You shall love thy neighbor, and hate your enemy. But I say to you, love your enemies, bless those who curse you, do good to those who hate you, and pray for those who spitefully use you and persecute you, that you may be the sons of your Father in heaven: for He maketh His sun rise on the evil and on the good, and sends rain on the just and on the unjust."

3.   Obey the Word of God. After you have repented for the un-forgiveness you have held in your heart, and prayed for the offending person then go and make it right! *(My statement "go and make it right" does not apply in instances where there has been any type of violence or abuse. Do not put your safety in jeopardy. Concentrate on your own personal healing and allow legal justice to do its job.)* In **Matthew 18:15-17**; we are encouraged to go and make it right with the person, who has offended us. You say, I have tried that, and the situation got worse. Guess what? I have too! Here's what I learned, when people are not ready to deal with the truth, they get what I like to call selective amnesia, or they deny the whole situation altogether. My friend, take heart God knows every detail surrounding the situation, and He is aware of your efforts to make peace (Romans 12:18).

114

We have no control over what other people do, but as Christians we responsible to respond in a manner that pleasing to God. He will reward your obedience. He is a God of justice and He has promised to take vengeance on your enemies (Isaiah 30:17-19; Deuteronomy 32:35; Romans 12:17-19). So after you have made every effort to make peace, focus on the promise, and believe God for restoration and restitution.

Deuteronomy 32:35–"Vengeance is Mine, and recompense; their foot shall slip in due time; For the day of their calamity is at hand, And the things to come hasten upon them.

Matthew 5:9-12- "Blesses are the peacemakers, for they shall be called the sons of God. Blessed are those who are persecuted for righteousness' sake, For theirs is the kingdom of heaven. "Blessed are you when they revile you and persecute you, and say all kinds of evil against you falsely for My sake. Rejoice and be exceedingly glad, for great is your reward in heaven, for so they persecuted the prophets who were before you.

Matthew 5:23-24 –"*Therefore if you bring your gift to the altar, and there remember that your brother has something against you, leave your gift there before the altar, and go your way. First be reconciled to your brother, and then come and offer your gift.*

Matthew 18:15-17- "Moreover if your brother sins against you, go and tell him his fault between you and him alone. If he hears you, you have gained your brother. But if he will not hear, take with you one or two more, that 'by the mouth of two or three witnesses every word may be established. And if he refuses to hear them, tell it to the church. But if he refuses even to hear the church, let him be to you like a heathen and a tax collector.

Romans 12:17-19 – *Repay no one evil for evil. Have regard for good things in the sight of all men. If it is possible, as much as depends on you, live peaceably with all men. Beloved, do not avenge yourselves, but rather give place to wrath; for it is written, "Vengeance is Mine, I will repay," says the Lord.*

Here's a Look at My Personal Forgiveness Checklist:

1. How do I feel when I hear that person or organization's name?

2. How do I respond when I hear someone speaking kindly, or negatively about that person or organization?

3. How do I feel and what is my immediate response when I see the person who has previously wronged me?

If you recognize that your responses do not line up with God's Word, and you still feel knots in your stomach, lumps in your throat, or fire from inside rising up the back of your neck, then let's face the facts, you are not over it! Continue to take the struggle to the Lord, He knows all of the details and He wants to heal your heart. My friend, in order for you, to receive the healing you need and live a fruitful life on this "Journey to Promise," you must let go of yesterday, which may involve taking a temporary loss and believing God to make it right in the end (Isaiah 54:17; Romans 8:28). He sees everything; nothing gets pass Him. He loves you, and He is faithful, please know the situation will be dealt with one way or another, leave that part to God and concentrate on your future (Philippians 3:14).

Here's A Sample Prayer on Forgiveness:

Lord, you are my Healer, and you have promised in your word, to heal the brokenhearted and bind up their wounds. Father, I ask you for the grace to forgive and to love again. Father, I pray that, by your Holy Spirit you will help me to release any, and all un-forgiveness, bitterness, wrath, anger, malice and clamor relating to (name the person and call out the action). Their actions (or inactions) have caused me pain and loss, but Lord I trust you and I look to you for restitution and restoration. Lord, I recognize that un-forgiveness is a sin, and it is my desire to live a life close to you and free from sin. Father, I repent for the sin that I have held in my heart towards (name the person). Lord, help me to be kind to other people, tenderhearted, and forgiving just as Christ forgave me, In Jesus name, Amen. **(Psalm 147:3; I John 1:9-10; Ephesians 4:31-32)**

If the situation calls for legal justice, first allow God to cleanse your heart and remove every trace of un-forgiveness and the offense. Then ask the Lord, for favor, guidance, and the right attorney. My friend, God is concerned about everyone involved and He has appointed ministers of authority to protect and execute justice in the earth (Romans 13). God is the ultimate Judge, and He is on the side of right (Isaiah 30:18), so take courage and embrace His favor. Your elder brother, Jesus Christ will be in court with you and He is the best defense attorney available (I John 2:1).

TRAVEL SECRET #2 - LEARN TO ACKNOWLEDGE GOD

Don't play trial and error with your life and the lives of those who depend on you for direction. When you need to select a spouse, an employee or an individual, to help you complete your mission, ask the Lord to give you direction in making that choice. He alone knows the heart, character, passion, motives, and abilities of a person. He has outlined your purpose. God has a suitable fit for your life and organization. When we acknowledge Him and learn how to wait on His guidance, the results will far exceed what you could have come up with on your own. I would suggest following the wisdom and example of Jesus Christ's disciples. When the disciples got ready to choose a replacement for Judas, the fallen disciple who betrayed Jesus, the Bible says, based on their perception and observation, they selected two men. The disciples believed both men to be well qualified to join in the leadership and Apostleship of the Church. The Bible says that after their preliminary selection was made, the disciples consulted God. The disciples understood that God alone knows what is in a person's heart, and He alone knows the ultimate plan for our lives (Acts 1:20-26).

You may be wondering if I am suggesting that we pray about everything. Yes, I am! **Proverbs 3:5-7** tells us to **"Trust in the LORD with all your heart, and lean not on your own understanding; <u>In all your ways acknowledge Him,</u> And He shall direct your paths. Do not be wise in your own eyes; Fear the LORD and depart from evil."** You have a choice. You can spend the time upfront in prayer about it or you can spend the time, energy, money, and tears trying to figure your way out of a mess! If you're smart, it will lead you back to God, and you'll learn one way or another that He's got the best plan - Jeremiah *29:11-"For I know the thoughts that I think toward you, says the LORD, thoughts of peace and not of evil, to give you a future and a hope."*

Failing to acknowledge the Lord in all your ways is a recipe for disaster. When making decisions that affect your future, the government, family, classroom, business, or church, Trial and Error is not the way to go! If people were all knowing and could figure out life on their own, they would not need the Lord or each other. The truth is we need Jesus and we need each other! We need His forgiveness, His wisdom, and His guidance. On our own, we have limited information and limited ability, and people lives and souls are at stake. Yes, yours, being the first and then the people with whom you are responsible. Dear friend, whatever plans you come up with on your own, will fall far below what Jesus Christ can give you. I suggest you spend some time consulting Him! In America, today, we are in need of revival, revitalization and great restoration. People are suffering in many ways across this country because someone in leadership failed to ask God for guidance. In their own personal pursuit for prestige, power, and financial gain, many leaders have neglected their responsibilities in the government, the business sector, school system, church and home. They have abused their God-given privilege and authority to lead and failed in their stewardship responsibilities.

When you are in a position of power, what you do and say, and what you refuse to do or say will affect someone else in a good or bad way. Leaders, I encourage you to watch your words. Learn how to use the power you have been given for good and don't attempt to carry the burden and responsibility of the people you lead on your own. Remember, God alone understands the needs of everyone in involved, and He is concerned about what's best for everyone. He has your best interest at heart and the people that you lead. In my experience and observation I have found that if you mishandle your position of stewardship, it will cost you, and if you are not truly repentant, you will eventually get replaced (Ezekiel 34:1-14).

TRAVEL SECRET #3 - DON'T BE A THIEF

The Tithe belongs to God; it is not yours to keep. If you choose to keep the tithe, you are considered a thief, and thieves do not sit in a position to be blessed!

Your **Offering** is a contribution given to the church for a particular purpose. The manner, in which you bring an offering to God, is just as important as the gift you're giving. The Lord does not want you to feel pressured in respect to a certain amount. He wants you to give according to your ability, willingly, with a good attitude and with an understanding of purpose.

2 Corinthians 9:6-8 -"But this I say: He who sows sparingly will also reap sparingly, and he who sows bountifully will also reap bountifully. So let each one give as he purposes in his heart, not grudgingly or of necessity; for God loves a cheerful giver. And God is able to make all grace abound toward you, that you, always having all sufficiency in all things, may have abundance for every good work."

Your **Tithe** is the tenth part of your personal income set apart as an offering to God for the support of the church, priesthood, or the like. The tithe is the only place in scripture where God invites the believer to test Him. He says, try it, trust me and obey me in this and I will prove My faithfulness in your life. In **Malachi 3:8-12**, the Bible explains the blessings that will accompany the believer's obedience and the curses that you open yourself up to if you choose to keep the tithe.

Malachi 3:8-12-"Will a man rob God? Yet you have robbed Me! But you say, in what have we robbed You?" "In tithes (first tenth) and offerings. You are curse with a curse, for you have robbed Me, even this whole nation. Bring all the tithes into the storehouse, that there may be food in My house, and try Me now in this," Says the Lord of hosts, "If I will not open for you the windows of heaven and pour out for you such blessing that there will not be room enough to receive it. And I will rebuke, the devour for your sakes, so that he will not destroy the fruit of your ground, nor shall the vine fail to bear fruit in the field," says the Lord of hosts; "And all nations will call you blessed, for you will be a delightful land," says the Lord of hosts."

1. The Lord says He will open up the windows of heaven and pour out for you such a blessings that there will not be room enough to receive it (Malachi 3:10).

2. The Lord says He will rebuke, which means He will sharply reprimand the enemy, Satan, for your sake. The Lord says He will protect you from the enemy and will protect the things that facilitate your progress and prosperity in life (Malachi 3:11).

3. The Lord says that you will experience pleasure, satisfaction, and enjoyment in life in such a way, that others around you will call you blessed (Malachi 3:12).

4. The Lord says that if you choose to keep the tithe and

offerings, in His eyes you are considered a thief and you are cursed with a curse. In your decision to disobey God's request of the tithe and offerings, you have opened the door to misfortune and removed yourself from the place and position of blessings and protection found in His promised Word (Malachi 3:8-18).

In my "Journey to Promise," I have observed that Christians withhold the **tithes and offerings** for one of four reasons: selfishness, fear, lack of trust in God's ability to take care of them, and lack of knowledge regarding the Word of God on the subject of tithes and offerings. In my opinion, you cannot afford not to tithe. It affects every area of your life, and without God's protection, Satan, your enemy, stands ready to bring trouble and destruction into your life.

John 10:9-12-"I am the door. If anyone enters by Me, he will be saved, and will go in and out and find pasture. The thief does not come except to steal, and to kill, and to destroy. I have come that they may have life, and that they may have it more abundantly. I am the good shepherd. The good shepherd gives His life for the sheep."

God has already given us His very best gift, His Son, Jesus Christ. The Lord, more than anyone else, understands your needs. The Lord wants to bless His children; after all, you represent Him. His request of the tithes and offerings is an issue of trust and obedience. In obedience, we position ourselves for the blessing. So, don't be a thief! Stay in the place of blessings and protection and bring ye **all the tithes and offerings** into the storehouse (church), so that the Gospel of Jesus Christ can continue to be preached unhindered. I encourage you to let generosity be the currency you should use on your "Journey to Promise."

TRAVEL SECRET #4 - WATCH YOUR MOUTH

One of the most powerful tools given to man is the spoken word. The right words spoken at the right time can save a person's life. The wrong words spoken in malice or anger can kill a relationship, a person's spirit, reputation, and influence in minutes! We can choose to use our words to be a positive influence in this society, or we can mishandle the God-given gift of words and become active participants in the chaos and drama that already exist in this world. When you chose to use your words in the right manner, they carry positive, creative ability. Your words can build up, encourage, and bring freedom, and knowledge to others.

King David in **Psalm 141:2-3** asked the Lord to set a watch; a guard over his mouth. He asked the Lord for help. King David understood that on his own, taming his tongue would be impossible, and he did not want to displease the Lord or open the door to evil into his life. *Psalm 141: 2-3–"Let my prayer be set forth before thee as incense; and the lifting up of my hands as the evening sacrifice. Set a watch, O LORD, before my mouth; keep the door of my lips. Incline not my heart to any evil thing, to practice wicked works with men that work iniquity: and let me not eat of their dainties."* On this journey with Christ, you would do well to follow King David's example. Guarding your mouth has to be a conscious and continual decision and you will need God's assistance. Our world is shaped either positively or negatively every day, by the very words that we allow to come out of our mouth. So it would be wise to make sure you are saying the right things (Proverbs 18:20-22; James 3:7-9). Guarding your mouth can be especially difficult when confusion and disorder exist in your environment. We all have something we could say, but not every thought that enters your mind should flow out of your mouth. When you are feeling pressed, frustrated, distressed, and troubled, those are the moments you should especially ask the Lord to help you guard your mouth. Complaining and negativity will hinder what God has promised you. In complaining, Satan, your enemy will capitalize, on the opportunity to usher strife and doubt into your heart and possibly walk off with your promise. Yes, and you will have helped in that destruction because you used your mouth to tear up and uproot your own prayers. This is where discretion becomes very valuable to your success on this journey. The *Merriam-Webster Dictionary* defines **Discretion** as **"the quality of being discreet, especially with reference to one's own actions or speech; prudence or decorum."** Knowing what to say or do and when to say it, can save you from a whole lot of heartache and headache. Remember, once those words come out of your mouth, they cannot be taken back. So pray and ask God to set a watch before your mouth that you may not sin with your lips! Speak the Word over the situation, instead of complaining. Speak life over your family and friends and watch God work miracles in your midst. The good and bad that can result from the words we speak is further explained in the following scriptures:

Psalm 34:11-15   *Proverbs 4:22-24*

Proverbs 19:10-12   *Matthew 5:17-19*

TRAVEL SECRET #5 - GOD LOVES YOU – Put Him First!

I would like to remind you that **God Loves You!** His love is genuine and unconditional. There is nothing that you can do to earn it or erase it. His love is not issued out or restrained based on your looks, talent, status, behavior, or checkbook. He simply loves you! It doesn't matter to Him if you're short, fat, skinny, or tall, broke and busted or rich and famous, **God Loves you!** He loves you, just the way you are with all your past mistakes, faults, potential and PROMISE! **God Loves You!** The Lord has promised, to never abandon you, or to leave you on your own without help or hope. I wish I could tell you that I've always believed that. The truth is it has taken years for me to accept and embrace God's unconditional love. Like many of you, I went looking for love in all the wrong places. Many times finding myself either poisoned or embittered by the company I kept. I was giving all my time and attention to idols. I was putting relationships, career, education and yes, even church work ahead of my relationship with Christ. I was on a mission to gain approval, position, acceptance and money. What's your mission? I had to hit rock bottom and lose all my stuff, friends and the like, to find out who was actually in my corner. Let me share something with you. When the dust settled, it was God and God alone! I went through some things that caused even my parents to take a step back. God allowed this out of His love for me. The Lord wanted me to understand that life without Him is not life; it's only mere existence. He wanted me to understand that there is no greater love to be found in Heaven or on earth than the love He has for me. When you understand that people's ability to control and manipulate you comes to a halt. God gave up what was most dear to Him, His only son, Jesus Christ, to save you and I, from Hell on earth and an eternity in Hell. Understanding God's love for you will put you in a position to embrace and appreciate the privileges and blessings of the life you've been given. God will help you forgive people who've hurt you. It may take several trips to the operating table, but if you are willing and you want to be free, God will remove every trace of un-forgiveness, bitterness, resentment, anger, rage and rejection. He will clean you up, inside and out, and then position you to help and protect other people. Yes, sometimes, even the very people who harmed you. (Read Genesis 37, Ch. 39-45) Restoration broke out in my life when I began to understand and embrace God's unconditional love and put Him first!

In April 2004, I accepted my God-given assignment to be a voice that would advocate for the poor and needy, one who would find practical ways to meet their needs and encourage others to do the same. I understand my assignment and the privilege I have been given to carry the Word of God to people in need of freedom and deliverance **(Psalm 82:3-4).** My first endeavor was a play called "Love Thy Neighbor", a message of God's love for people. I remember being faced with many challenges, wondering if I'd be able to complete the task, being a single parent with no family in the city. Then, I watched God put a group of anointed, gifted, and dedicated actors, workers and musicians, together. All of the play's budgetary needs were met. I remember souls coming to the altar when that production ended. What stands out most is something I heard the Lord, by His Holy Spirit say to me before even one rehearsal or meeting had taken place. "He said, stop waiting for the cheerleaders to come... they are not coming. I am all you need and I have already voted for your success." For a person, who had spent most of her life searching for approval, acceptance, and fighting fear, I cannot fully explain how my heart felt when I heard God say, "I have already voted for your success." The same God that created the heavens and the earth had asked me to do something, and then before I could even start the task, He told me, "I have already voted for your success." Amazing!

My friend and fellow traveler, when you reach a place, on

your journey, where things seem dark and lonely, trust God, believe Him, and put Him first because He really loves you! He has an awesome plan for your life, and His heart towards you involves blessings, and increase. He wants you to know that you are chosen, accepted and forgiven (Ephesians 1:3-7). He wants you to know that His grace, redemption and restoring power is available to you. Don't look for validation or shelter in people, positions, things or status, because those things will fail. Believe **GOD LOVES YOU – Put Him First** and you will find out like me that God's love is more than enough!

God's love for you will never change! - **(Romans 8:37-39)**

God will never leave or abandon you! - **(Hebrews 13:5)**

*God is love***! - (I John 4:8)**

God made a tremendous sacrifice, His son Jesus and Jesus

Sacrificed His life, all out of love for you! **–(Romans 5:8)**

God Loves You – Put Him First!

TRAVEL SECRET #6 - BE ON THE LOOKOUT FOR PRIDE!

Be on the lookout for **pride.** It's subtle. It will creep up on you and everyone, except you will know you're prideful!

Pride will keep you in lack because you are ashamed to go to the food pantry or to take a job that you consider being beneath you, not considering your responsibilities or the needs of your family. Some people would prefer to go without, make excuses, leech off of others, and even steal to continue their facade; putting on the appearance that things are much better than what they really are. When people refuse to ask for help or make the necessary changes needed to make life better for themselves and those they are responsible for, pride is the culprit. Pride can cause strain and turmoil in your relationships, especially when you refuse to say three simple words... "I am sorry; I was wrong, please forgive me," when it's needed. Pride is why many business, churches, and marriages have failed. Prideful people insist on having things their way, all the time, and they refuse to compromise or look for ways to work together. In my opinion, pride strengthens the hands abuse, misconduct and dysfunction and gives that poison permission to continue to infect others. Prideful people deliberately keep secrets and cover things up because they are selfish and more concerned about image, and less concerned with truth and doing what is right and fair! Pastor Carolyn Cofield **(see - Chapter 5)** wrote a book called *"Tell the Truth and Shame the Devil"* that discusses the freedom found when truth is revealed. I know personally that when you expose the issue, its power is diminished, and you then sit in a place where healing, deliverance, and restoration can begin.

Pride is extremely dangerous. It binds and blinds. It's a tool of bondage sent straight from the pit of Hell! Many people will miss heaven because they refuse to acknowledge their need for Jesus Christ. Many people are suffering now or have suffered way too long because they were scared to go to the altar and ask for prayer. They are too scared to go talk to the pastor about their personal struggles, too scared to ask for help! They are too ashamed, too proud, and too concerned about what others think. The *Merriam-Webster Dictionary* defines **Pride** as "**a high or inordinate opinion of one's own dignity, importance, merit or superiority, whether as cherished in the mind or as displayed in bearing conduct, etc.**" We are all important to God, and whatever gifts, talents, intellect, abilities, blessings, and privileges we have, we have because of God's GRACE. Not because, He loves some of us more than others, we're all equally valuable to God. We are all His favorites! We have been given what we have based on our assignments in the earth.

It's about building His kingdom, not our own ship. It's about being a blessing because we've been blessed! It's about showcasing the grace, mercy and the love of God in the earth. It's about Him, not you and your stuff. So, if you think you are better than your brother, think again! If you are more concerned about maintaining a certain image and the opinions of people than living in the truth and the liberty that Christ has afforded you, pride is your friend. God wants you to be free physically, mentally, emotionally, financially, and spiritually. On this "Journey to Promise," you will have many opportunities to meet with Pride. Refuse his company and don't let him steal your promise and usurp your destiny! Satan was excommunicated from Heaven and doomed to an eternity in Hell because of pride. Our Father in Heaven is a loving God and He wants so much to bless His children, but if we choose to operate in pride His wrath is sure to come. So be on the lookout for Pride!

Proverbs 11:1-3-"A false balance is abomination to the LORD: but a just weight is his delight. When pride cometh, then cometh shame: but with the lowly is wisdom. The integrity of the upright shall guide them: but the perverseness of transgressors shall destroy them."

Proverbs 16:17-19-"The highway of the upright is to depart from evil: he the keepeth his way preserveth his soul. Pride goeth before destruction, and a haughty spirit before a fall. Better it is to be of a humble spirit with the lowly, than to divide the spoil with the proud."

Proverbs 29:23-"A man's pride shall bring him low: but honor shall uphold the humble in spirit."

TRAVEL SECRET #7 - DON'T LINGER in the VALLEY OF THE SHADOW OF DEATH
A PLACE CRAFTED TO STEAL YOUR PROMISE

The **Bermuda Triangle** is a region in the northwestern Atlantic Ocean where a number of aircrafts and surface vessels have allegedly disappeared without a trace, never to be seen again. On this Journey to Promise, we have a similar territory called the **Valley of the Shadow of Death.** In the **Valley of the Shadow of Death**, Satan will attempt to introduce and nurture negative and dangerous emotions into

136

your life. These negative emotions are unproductive and time robbers. They'll sap your energy and steal your joy. If you linger, get side tracked or distracted in the **Valley of the Shadow of Death**, you will literally watch your physical health, your mental health, your marriage, your family, your money, your dreams, your purpose, and your promises from God disappear, right in front of your face. Hanging out in the **Valley of the Shadow of Death** will keep you from receiving what God has for you on this "Journey to Promise."

Before I go any further, there are two things I want you to remember about being in the **Valley of the Shadow of Death: 1.** It is just a shadow and **2.** God is with you! In my research, I found three distinct definitions for the word **Shadow:**

Defense

A slight suggestion

To overspread with shade or darkness; to cast gloom over

On this journey, you will run into *darkness.* On occasion, the situation from your point of view may seem grim and hopeless. Sometimes people and the situations may *slightly suggest* that your promise from God was a mere figment of your imagination and what you see now is all you will ever have or become, but that Devil is a LIE! Hope in God! Satan, your enemy, is trying to paint a picture in your mind, because he wants you to get stuck and bewildered by the gloom and the overcast of your current situation (I Peter 5:8). He wants you to take your eyes off of Jesus Christ, your Help, your Keeper, your Redeemer, your Advocate, and **Defender!** God is the only one who ever promised to be with you in the good and the bad times. His love is stronger than every opposing force you will ever come across! In **Psalm 23:4**, the psalmist says, *"I will not fear any evil."* Why, because God is with me, and He has given me His rod **(His Word; His instruction)** and His staff **(His support and guidance)** to get me through this part of the journey.

> *Psalm 23:4 –"Yea, though I walk through the valley of the shadow of death, I will fear no evil; For you are with me; Your rod and Your staff they comfort me."*

God has prepared rivers of blessings with your name on it, but those blessings cannot flow freely into your life or through your life into others when you hang around with the residents of the **Valley of the Shadow of Death**. On my

"Journey to Promise," I have encountered the following Valley Residents:

ANXIETY	**DEPRESSION**	**DISCOURAGEMENT**
REGRET	**REJECTION**	**DISAPPOINTMENT**
FAILURE	**FEAR**	

Do not be fooled. You cannot pray effectively or operate in your God-given authority with all that baggage. If you are going to walk in the purpose and promises of God, and escape the **Valley of the Shadow of Death** you must arm yourself with the Word of God. Only the Word of God can secure your freedom and escape from the **Valley of the Shadow of Death.** Maintaining that victory will require that you first believe and accept that God loves and values you (Jeremiah 33:3). You are a marvelous work of God's hands, and you are fearfully and wonderfully made in His image (Psalm 139:14 and Genesis 1:26). You were born to reign in this life, not to be misused or abused. You must make a decision to get connected with a local church where the whole Word of God is preached on a regular basis. Then make it a point to spend some time talking to God on a daily basis and searching the scriptures that pertain to your issue specifically. Read, memorize, and quote those scriptures aloud until the Word of

God takes root in your heart and faith springs forth in your life. If you find that you are still struggling in some areas, run to God, He created you. Be honest with Him about where you are inside and simply ask the Lord to help you. If the process seems to be overwhelming, don't be prideful, get help, consult a qualified, credible counselor or minister and let them help you decipher through and out of the mess.

Let's talk about some things you and I can do to avoid getting stuck and stranded in the **Valley of the Shadow of Death.**

Frustration, discouragement, and disappointment can occur when your present reality is not what you anticipated or hoped for. These emotions can also surface when the promise or breakthrough is taking much longer than you expected. Beware, these are moments where you must make every effort to hold on to what God's Word has to say about the issue because if you begin to complain about your circumstances, doubt is inevitable and doubt will keep you from receiving the promises of God.

Disappointment and regret can also occur when you recognize that you have squandered precious opportunities to better your life or improve your current situation. It happens when you know deep down inside that you really did not give it your all, or that for whatever reason you got distracted from the assigned task. The deception here is that some people still believe the outcome is still going to be okay. For example, college students who have not attended classes or completed their assignments on time, but seem to be shocked when the grades are released, and they've been put on academic probation or told to leave school. Distraction will always cost you something! Usually, A lot more than you planned on paying. Remember, you have help in Jesus Christ! He has the ability to restore what you have lost, when you learn how to do things God's way. The restoration process can begin the moment you repent and ask God to help you move forward differently.

Solution: **Ephesians 6:10-18-"Finally, my brethren, be strong in the Lord and in the power of His might. Put on the whole armor of God, that you may be able to stand against the wiles of the devil. For we do not wrestle against flesh and blood, but against principalities, against powers, against the rulers of the darkness of this age, against spiritual hosts of wickedness in the heavenly places. Therefore take up the whole armor of God, that you may be able to withstand in the evil day, and having done all, to stand. Stand therefore, having girded your waist with truth, having put on the breastplate of righteousness,** *and having shod your feet with the preparation of the gospel of peace; above all, taking the shield of faith with which you will be able to quench all the fiery darts of the wicked one. And take the helmet of salvation, and the sword of the Spirit, which is the word of God; praying always with all prayer and supplication in the Spirit, being watchful to this end with all perseverance and supplication for all the saints"*

If you find yourself in the dark pit of **Depression, Anxiety, and Hopelessness,** it's probably because things in your life are out of order and out of control and somehow you've bought into the lie that things will never change. It's a lie, sent straight from the pit of hell. A LIE! You were born with the gift of choice! You can spend the rest of your life blaming others or you can make some hard decisions, refuse to tolerate the mess, and do whatever is necessary to obtain your emotional, mental, and spiritual freedom. Yes, it is easy to get stuck playing the victim. I know personally that nursing your injuries and complaining requires far less courage and effort than standing on the Word of God, standing up for yourself, refusing the negative, and demanding respect. You can also opt to walk around in denial and pretend if you want, but your mess will find a way to surface. Our unresolved issues and fears will usually show up in some other type of negative or compulsive behavior. We overeat, shop excessively because we're trying to fill a hole, a void and we are eating, spending and buying more because we feel less or not in control of other areas of our lives. Not to mention the gambling, alcoholism, lying, drug use and other immoral acts people participate in search of that endorphin rush, or escape, anything to feel better. Some of our mental and physical conditions can be linked to unresolved issues, and then there's the subtle deceiver called busyness. Working hard on other people's problems and no time to work on your own stuff or just making work, in general; your escape, to avoid some things altogether. If you want to be emotionally and mentally free, you need to quit giving other people the control dial in your life. God put you on this earth, promised that He would never leave you, nor forsake you and then left you a life manual, His Holy Word. It's your responsibility to find out what He has to say about your life. Your happiness is not someone else's responsibility. It's a decision that you make (Proverbs 3:13-14). It can be attained and maintained when you first learn to accept that God is in charge, and He has the best plan for your life (Psalm 31:41-16; Jeremiah 29:11). Begin to give other people and things proper value in your life. The Lord had to teach me that my value was not in someone else's opinion of me. It was not in my job title or position, not in the degrees I've obtained

143

or the lack thereof, or in the numbers on my paycheck or the lack thereof. *I'm valuable because God saw a need for me in the earth and His word says, "I am fearfully and wonderfully made.... A marvelous work of His hands - Psalm 139:14."* I have stood in my bathroom mirror, and I have walked through my house many days quoting this exact scripture. God, my Father and creator, used this simple phrase to restore my self-esteem.

Please do not misunderstand what I am saying, when you or an individual you know is are suffering from depression, anxiety or hopelessness, mental health counseling can prove to be highly beneficial. Sometimes, we need the help of a qualified professional or minister to help us decipher through and out of the messy stuff, but when all the counseling is done, and all the medications have been given out if God doesn't step in, deliverance and freedom will not come.

Sin is the root cause of most of our issues; the sins we've willingly committed or sins committed against us (Deuteronomy 28). I speak as one who spent far, far too many days in the pit of despair and one who has been set free from the **Valley of the Shadow of Death** by the grace and power of God. The liberty Christ bought on the cross with His blood can be obtained with pure repentance. You need to take ownership for your part in the mess, the sins you've committed and forgive those who have wronged you and then repent. Repentance is a change of mind and a decision to follow God's directives. Life is too short. The Promise is too close, and God is too good to get stuck in the **Valley of the Shadow of Death**. Make a decision today, to Choose Life! Allow the bad things of your yesterday to die. Believe in what God has to say about you! When it all comes down to it, where you stand with Him is what truly matters. Making a daily list **(mentally or literally)** of the things you are thankful for, and making an effort to look for the good around you, instead of the negative, can birth an attitude of thanksgiving and praise. I dare you to try it. It will change how you see yourself and the world around you.

*Solution: **Philippians 3:13-15-"Brethren, I do not count myself to have apprehended; but one thing I do, forgetting those things which are behind and reaching forward to those things which are ahead, I press toward the goal for the prize of the upward call of God in Christ Jesus. Therefore let us, as many as are mature, have this mind; and if in anything you think otherwise, God will reveal even this to you."***

Philippians 4:8-"Finally, brethren, whatever things are true, whatever things are noble, whatever things are just, whatever things are pure, whatever things are lovely, whatever things are of good report, if there is any virtue and if there is anything praiseworthy--meditate on these things."

Fear, Failure, and Rejection are the ultimate assassins sent from the pit of hell, to shut you down and render you powerless and unusable in the Kingdom of God. There is a pain and anger that accompanies rejection that only God can heal. Honestly, I cannot even put into words how much it hurts inside when you have given your heart, time, energy, money, and talents to a particular organization, a marriage or a project, only to be told in some manner or another, "NOT GOOD ENOUGH!" Sometimes, what you hear is, "You are NOT good enough, not smart enough, not pretty enough, not skinny enough, not wealthy enough, not social enough, not popular enough, or talented enough. Not you, not now!" From rejection, I learned that God heals **all wounds.** Only He controls my future, not parents, not my boss, not my pastor, not my teachers, not my family, not my friends, and certainly, not my enemies. I had to learn how to give the Lord all the broken pieces of my heart and take Him at His Word and promise to restore my soul. Sorry to say, it has taken years;

because there was no coach, or mentor explaining to me what I needed to do, to get over this hurdle. I first learned that I had to be honest about my pain and then lay it all on the altar **(and not go back and pick it up again in my conversations).** Then, I had to make a choice **(and it is a choice)** to forgive the people who hurt me and trust God with my restitution and restoration. I had learned how to believe again, and not allow the fear of being hurt and disappointed paralyze me and keep me from trying and trusting again. I had to take ownership for my failures, and repent. I recognized that some opportunities were mishandled. I then asked the Lord to cleanse me from all those self-sabotaging tendencies. I stood on God's Word for healing and restoration of my soul. God gave me hope and strength to embrace His promises again. I had to let go of yesterday. I had to stop rehearsing who did what, when, and truly forgive. Honestly, I spent many nights crying out to God to help me forgive, to help me move on, and to **Restore My soul!**

My friends, God gave me a promise in the **Valley of the Shadow of Death,** a promise of Restoration! When I felt like a failure and my life looked like a waste dump; God whispered, Hope! I was hurt, confused, distraught and disappointed with life, and with people, **BUT GOD,** in His

147

awesome Grace caused me to live, taught me to pray, and made me stronger.

My personal promise of restoration: *Isaiah 51:1-3-* *"Hearken to me, ye that follow after righteousness, ye that seek the LORD: look unto the rock whence ye are hewn, and to the hole of the pit whence ye are digged. Look unto Abraham your father, and unto Sarah that bare you: for I called him alone, and blessed him, and increased him. For the LORD shall comfort Zion: he will comfort all her waste places; and he will make her wilderness like Eden, and her desert like the garden of the LORD; joy and gladness shall be found therein, thanksgiving, and the voice of melody."*

Dear friend and fellow journeyman; the reason behind our deliverance boils down to God's love for us and our service to Him. All the promises of God are yes and amen (2 Corinthians 1:20)! Jesus Christ came and sacrificed His life to secure your **Peace and Deliverance!** Don't get stuck in the **Valley of the Shadow of Death.** Don't allow yourself to get sidetracked by **Fear, Failure and Rejection.** Remember, your promise, and your destiny could be jeopardized and delayed if you get stranded on the side of the road in the **Valley of the Shadow of Death** behind **disappointment, un-forgiveness and regret. I encourage you today to ----**

Push pass the **FEAR** - if need be do it scared, Just don't allow **FEAR** to dictate your actions!

Take off the cloak of **REJECTION** and trust God to bring you into places where you are **CELEBRATED** and not just **TOLERATED!**

TRY again, **LIVE** again, and **BELIEVE** again and **PRAISE** God, because He gives **DO-OVERS!**

DON'T LET FAILURE WIN!

Travel Secrets

Saving you Time, Money, and Heartache

Travel Secret #1 - Choose to Forgive

Travel Secret #2 - Learn to Acknowledge God

Travel Secret #3 - Don't Be a Thief

Travel Secret #4 - Watch Your Mouth

Travel Secret #5 - God Loves You- Put Him First

Travel Secret #6 - Be On the Lookout for Pride

Travel Secret #7 - Don't Linger in the Valley of the Shadow of Death

Chapter 7

My Place of Promise

"Listen to Me, you who follow after righteousness, you who seek the Lord: look to the rock from which you were hewn, and to the hole of the pit from which you were dug. Look to Abraham your father, and to Sarah who bore you; for I called him alone, and blessed him and increased him." For the Lord will comfort Zion, He will comfort all her waste places; He will make her wilderness like Eden, And her desert like the garden of the Lord; Joy and gladness will be found in it, thanksgiving and the voice of melody."

Isaiah 51:1-3

The promise of unconditional love, rescue, reconciliation and relationship, is the greatest promise anyone could have ever made to me. My life on earth now restored and redeemed. My death sentence in Hell erased and pardoned because I choose to believe that God exists and that His son; Jesus Christ paid the penalty for my sins.

I have known sin and all of the turmoil and devastation that it can cause. Had it not been for the grace and sovereignty of an Almighty God and the prayers of many people, my futile search for acceptance, approval and love would have surely ended in death and destruction. On my journey, Jesus Christ found me, pursued me and saved my life and now I understand mercy. I understand real love. I know how it feels to be accepted, and the Lord has already voted for my success. So I can rest, God's got my back, He is my help, and He will keep His promises!

In 1994, I reluctantly gave up homeownership in a divorce for the sake of my sanity, and my safety. The Lord, during that divorce, gave me a promise of restoration.

Isaiah 51:1-3 –"Listen to Me, you who follow after righteousness, you who seek the Lord; Look to the rock from which you were hewn, and to the hole of the pit from which you were dug. Look to Abraham your father, and to Sarah who bore you; for I called him alone, and blessed him and increased him. For the Lord will comfort Zion, He will comfort all her waste places; He will make her wilderness like Eden, and her desert like the garden of the Lord; Joy and gladness will be found in it, thanksgiving and the voice of melody."

The Lord promised to comfort all my waste places, and He just that. The ruins have been rebuilt! My heart healed, my soul redeemed, and my life restored! Over the years, I have watched the Lord put my faith, heart, and life back together. I am a Blessed Black Woman! I am married to a brilliant man, and we have two beautiful, healthy, and productive children. The Lord has given us a wonderful home and the means to maintain it. In July 2007, my husband and I leased a house with an option to buy. Ten months into the lease, the owner said the mortgage was too high for her and that she was letting the house go. I was devastated and angry. My family and I were suddenly thrown into a terrible situation due to the negligence or mismanagement of someone else. This bump in the road was not something that anyone could have ever anticipated. Homelessness was not ever a thought. We had done our part. We paid our rent on time and took good care of the property. Still, on the other end of the phone was someone saying, "You can stay in the house until it goes into foreclosure and they kick you out!" We made a decision to continue to honor our portion of the lease agreement. Setting a defense against any future accusation that we could have caused this situation. After meeting with an attorney and talking to the bank that held the loan on the property, we were instructed to stop paying because the situation was beyond repair. Continuing to pay the owner would profit nothing. Understanding that moving was something we now needed to consider; we began to pay rent to ourselves.

Initially, I was not very concerned about staying in this house, but I knew that God had a home for us somewhere. We needed a certain amount of square feet. We wanted to stay in the same school district because my youngest child was now in high school. We needed space to minister to people, and this blended family needed a place to call home. It was time to invest in our own future instead of making the landlord rich. We needed a home of our own! For years, I had held dear these scriptures concerning provision and housing:

Proverbs 19:14 - House and riches are the inheritance of fathers: and a prudent wife is from the LORD.

Psalm 24:1 – The earth is the Lord's, and the fullness thereof; the world, and they that dwell therein.

Philippians 4:19 – But my God shall supply all your need according to his riches in glory by Christ Jesus.

Homeownership for the Sanders Family was about believing in the promises of God. First of all, I am a child of the Most High God, the creator of heaven and earth, is my Father and He has promised to meet all my needs (Philippians 4:19).

Secondly, according to Psalm 24:1 everything belongs to Him, and He can give me whatever He chooses (Psalm 47:3-4), and no one on earth and no devil in Hell can stop Him! Finally, I am the spiritual seed of Abraham, because of my faith in God and His Son, Jesus Christ, and houses and land are part of my covenant inheritance (Genesis 22:17-18). Reggie and I made a decision to believe God. We asked the Lord to work this situation out in our favor and give us a home. We continued to move forward in the practice of tithing; good stewardship of the property and we remained thankful, understanding that God had already done a great deal for us. I remember walking the property line praying, and asking the Lord to show us and lead us to the space and place on this earth that He had assigned and set aside for us. My husband, Reggie had a complete stance on the issue. While I could believe that God had a place for us, Reggie stood on what the Lord had spoken to him specifically about this piece of land from the first day until the day we closed on the property. A modern day example of unwavering faith in action, I on the other hand, packed the house twice *(everything except Reggie's stuff because he was adamant that this was the home for us, and he was not making any plans to move).* I even put a deposit down on another place, but each time I went into prayer about our housing, I was always instructed to stay put and prompted several times to read the following scriptures:

155

Jeremiah 31:38-40-"Behold, the days are coming says the Lord, that the city shall be built for the Lord from the Tower of Hananel to the Corner Gate. The surveyor's line shall again extend straight toward Goath. And the whole valley of the dead bodies and of the ashes, and all the fields as far as the brook of Kidron, to the corner of the Horse Gate toward the east, shall be holy to the Lord, it shall not be plucked up or thrown down anymore forever."

Jeremiah 32:15-17-"For thus says the Lord of host, the God of Israel; "Houses and fields and vineyards shall be possessed again in this land. Now when I delivered the purchase deed to Baruch the son of Neriah, I prayed to the Lord, saying; Ah Lord God! Behold, You have made the heavens and the earth by Your great power and outstretched arm. There is nothing too hard for You."

Now I understand that this scripture was given to the prophet Jeremiah, personally, and it pertained to the circumstances of his day, but if you've ever been homeless or evicted, **(Like me)** these scriptures carry a far greater weight. In reading the phrases: ***"not plucked up or thrown down anymore forever"*** *and "There is nothing too hard for God."* I recognized that God wanted to provide stability for us. The Lord's heart concerning the matter involved taking legal possession of the home; we were already in. So what did we do? We stayed put. We stayed put, despite the eviction notices, the auction at the courthouse steps, three court proceedings, and several meetings with lawyers, brokers, real estate agents and the bank; all in the midst of trying to assist three different family members, all of whom lived out of town. During this three-year journey to home ownership, both of my husband's parents and my mother had suffered strokes. The pressure was on, and our faith was being stretched, but God was faithful. In the midst of this storm, God gave us the grace and the ability to maintain and grow a business. To provide some degree of stability and security for our two children, and to take care for our elderly parents. The Lord allowed a situation in our lives that seemed extremely hard most days, and because this storm went on for so long we were able to accumulate a sizable deposit by paying rent to ourselves. On June 15, 2011, we used that money as a down payment on the exact home the Lord had promised from the beginning. We learned, as a family that God is a Provider and a Sustainer. He willingly gives you the strength and grace needed for every task, and for every part of the journey. The Lord keeps His promises, and His Word stands as the final authority. When the real estate agent and our own lawyer questioned whether or not we could afford the house, I watched God give us favor both in court while attempting to exercise our renter's rights, and in the closing process, along with money in the bank. God did it! He, in His mercy and tender loving care, provided a safe, stable and lovely place for my family, and I to live. It's in a nice community with good neighbors. God granted us favor! God made the provision! God gave us the house and the land and my mortgage is less than the rent I use to pay. **"Is there anything too hard for God (Jeremiah 32:27b)?"**

Psalm 44:1-3-"We have heard with our ears, O God, Our fathers have told us, The deeds You did in their days in days of old; You drove out the nations with Your hand, But them You planted; You afflicted the peoples, and cast them out. For they did not gain possession of the land by their own sword, Nor did their own arm save them. But it was Your right hand, Your arm and the light of Your countenance. Because You favored them."

The Bible has been my sustaining source. God, my Father and your creator is concerned about every aspect of your life, and more than anything else He wants a close relationship with you. So, take your own personal "Journey to Promise," with Him, and don't forget to invite Jesus Christ along for the ride. Find out what the Word of God has to say about your life, health, wealth, family, and purpose, and then only believe.

Have faith in God; trust in His ability, and wait on His promise. Obey and cooperate with Him and He shall bring it to pass, *"that you may be called trees of righteousness, the planting of the Lord, that He might be glorified (Isaiah 61:3b)."*

Prayer is the Key,

Faith is the Vehicle,

And

Patience is the Road that leads to

God's manifested Glory!

REFERENCES

Hayford, Jack W., Litt. D *New Spirit-Filled Life Bible -NKJV.*
Tennessee: Thomas Nelson, Inc. 2002

Strong, James., S.T.D, LL.D *The Exhaustive Concordance of the
Bible with the Dictionaries of Hebrew and Greek Words.*
Massachusetts: Hendrickson Publishers

Wilkinson, Bruce H., *The Prayer of Jabez.* Oregon: Multnomah
Publishers, Inc. 2000

http://www.biblegateway.com

http://www.merriam-webster.com

http://www.census.gov/compendia/statb/2012/table/12s1
103.pdf

ABOUT THE AUTHOR

Minister LaDonna K. Sanders is a woman of prayer, a gifted administrator, a Psalmist, a Drama Director, an actress, and a Writer from Kansas City, Kansas. She graduated from Kansas City Kansas Community College with an Associates of Arts in Liberal Arts and also attended Oral Roberts University in Tulsa, Oklahoma. Minister Sanders obtained her second Associates Degree in Practical Theology from Mid-Hudson Bible Institute of Poughkeepsie, NY. During her time in Tulsa, Oklahoma, she was privileged to work for and serve the late Pastor Billy Joe Daugherty and his wife Pastor Sharon Daugherty of Victory Christian Center. In May 2004, she received her licensed as a Minister under Bishop Gary McIntosh of Tulsa, Oklahoma where she also served as the Special Events Coordinator and on the Frontline Worship Team at Greenwood Christian Center.

Hope in Jesus Christ is the fundamental message of her writings, drama skits, plays, and music. Her written works include two stage-plays, "Love Thy Neighbor" and "Penalty Paid," and two skits called, "The Lord Our Righteousness" and "The Jeweler's Treasure". Included in the back of this book is a single from her latest musical project. The title of the song is taken from Psalm 42:8 - "A Prayer to the God of My Life."

Minister LaDonna K. Sanders now lives in Upstate New York with her husband of 8 years, Rev. Reginald P. Sanders, Jr., and their two children Brian and Jahmani.

CD Included: "Psalm 42:8 – A Prayer to the God of My Life" ©2011
Lyrics: LaDonna K Sanders
Pianist: Tyrone Hartzog
Mixed: Andre Surgrick

For Additional Copies of this Book
Contact:
Kayla Publishing
P O Box 945
Guilderland, NY 12084-0945
www.kaylapublishing.com
Inspirational Books, Music and More

New Book Release - Fall 2013
"Healing Waters"
By LaDonna K. Sanders
66 Days of Faith Building Truth,
To Help You Reclaim Your Healing!